THE
CONFIDENCE
FACTOR

THE CONFIDENCE FACTOR

The seven secrets of successful people

Annie Ashdown

crimson

The Confidence Factor: The seven secrets of successful people

This edition first published in Great Britain in 2013 by Crimson Publishing Ltd, The Tramshed, Walcot Street, Bath BA1 5BB

British Library Cataloguing in Publication Data
A catalogue record for this book is available from the British Library

ISBN 978 1 78059 167 4

Typeset by IDSUK (DataConnection) Ltd
Printed and bound in the UK by Bell & Bain Ltd, Glasgow

My wish for every reader:

'Promise me you will always remember you are braver than you believe and stronger than you seem and smarter than you think.'

Christopher Robin to Pooh

A. A. Milne

CONTENTS

Contents

Contents

ACKNOWLEDGEMENTS

Dad
This book is dedicated to my father, who taught me:

There is no such word as can't.
Get straight back up after every knock-back.
Do not wait for opportunities – create them.
It is never about what life throws at you, but how you deal with it.
Always believe in your dreams and never quit.
Always be yourself.
Never lower your standards.

Dad, thank you – you walked your talk as you overcame endless setbacks. Your words gave me an inner strength to keep going. I miss you every day.

A special thank you to my wonderful editors, Jon Finch and Hugh Brune – and all the team at Crimson Publishing, especially Abby Coften.

Thank you also to Sharon Walker.
Thank you Fiona Lindsay and all the team at Limelight Celebrity Management.

A heartfelt thank-you to each contributor and client for sharing so openly and honestly.

Thank you to all my past and present clients who I feel are superstars for investing time in themselves.

Acknowledgements

Thank you Peter, Lesley, David, Amanda, Steph, Dan and Alex – for championing me, loving me, supporting me and being the wind beneath my wings.

Thanks to my wonderful tribe – you are simply the very best. You know who you are.

'If you were absent during my struggles, do not expect
to be present during my success.'

Will Smith

Part 1. Getting ready to change

'I had to know and understand my own story before I could listen to and help other people with theirs.'

President Barack Obama

Chapter 1

INTRODUCTION

I have studied the habits of successful people for many years. Let me tell you, they are regular people who have flaws, shortcomings and defects, and experience challenges and bad days. However, having inner confidence means they don't let any of this hold them back. In this book you will find real-life case studies, invaluable insights and inspiring stories from well-known high achievers to demonstrate how they built self-confidence and enabled success.

When I was lacking in confidence, people-pleasing and wrapped in fear, I didn't realise how much power the fear had over me because I was feeding it. Not everyone wants to become a world leader, but with confidence, charisma and courage you can become a leader in your own world. Confidence is essential to your performance in the workforce and an essential component in creating and maintaining healthy relationships.

I am not suggesting you become a performing seal, an angel, or change who you fundamentally are. However, I am suggesting you assimilate, process and apply the 'seven secrets' so you can begin to identify and trust your own instincts and enhance your strengths to create the life you want.

> The Confidence Factor is the elixir of my journey so far. I hope it will inspire, motivate and support each and every one of you on your journey. I wish you love, laughter and light.
>
> Annie — The Confidence Expert

Is this book for you?

There are no short-cuts to any place worth going, so this book is not a quick fix. However, it's easy to read without being too conceptual.

The Confidence Factor will help you regardless of what you do or don't do for a living. It doesn't matter whether you are an athlete, a CEO, a salesperson, an entrepreneur, a lawyer, a fashion designer, a hairdresser, a corporate employee, an actress, a teacher, a nurse, a teenager, a masseuse, an interior designer or a banker. Confidence, or the lack of it, is an issue that affects all of us. I have had the pleasure of interviewing several successful people who embody the seven secrets in their daily life, and have peppered these interviews throughout the book. They include Jo Fairley, co-founder of Green & Black's, Sam Roddick, founder of Coco De Mer, the legendary Lynne Franks, Carla Buzai, editor of *The Huffington Post* UK, Judy Piatkus, founder of Piatkus Books, and ITV agony aunt, *This Morning*'s Denise Robertson, MBE.

How will this book benefit you?

You will learn how to:

- create personal effectiveness both personally and professionally
- focus on your strengths
- be more assertive
- maximise your potential
- raise your confidence and self-esteem
- develop your courage muscles
- communicate effectively with tricky people professionally or personally
- become more productive and strategic
- nurture the relationship with yourself
- overcome stress and anxiety
- ask for what you want
- become aware and develop your intuition

- say no with confidence and ease
- change the way you think about yourself
- define your own reality and not buy into everyone else's
- witness your own thoughts without judging them
- understand that your perception of others is a reflection of yourself and that your reaction to yourself is your awareness of yourself.

Annie's quiz. Are you lacking in the confidence factor?

Not everyone who lacks confidence is aware of how much stronger and happier they could be if they made a decision to take control of their lives. Take this quick quiz to see if there is room for improvement in your own life. Think about the questions carefully and answer truthfully based on how things actually are for you today, not how you think they should be. There are no right or wrong answers – only honest or dishonest ones.

- Are you on the right road to get to where you want to be, or are you hanging around on this road because it is safe and familiar?
- Do you have a strategy, a map, a timeline and a set of life-skills?
- Do you know the rules to success?
- Can you honestly say you are accountable for all your choices, behaviour and actions, or do you allow yourself to be manipulated and seduced into what others think is good for you?
- Do you have focus and daily discipline?
- Do you people-please in relationships at the expense of your own happiness?
- Are you building your dream, work-wise, or being hired to build someone else's?
- Do you feel anxious about giving a presentation at work?
- Do you feel awkward asking your boss directly for a rise?

- Have you ever felt intimidated around a troublesome neighbour?
- Have you ever lost your voice or talked too much at interviews?
- Do you believe you must always be understanding, even when others are disrespectful of you?
- Do you feel uncomfortable setting a boundary with your teen/sibling/partner/boss, or in saying no?
- Do you want everyone to like and approve of you?
- Do you find yourself making excuses for someone's bad behaviour?
- Do you find the 'bad boys' or 'bad girls' attractive?
- Do you avoid confrontation?
- Do you procrastinate around changing careers, or starting a business?
- Do you feel deflated when rejected by a partner?
- Do you feel you are not smart enough, slim enough, tall enough, funny enough?
- Do you feel uncomfortable asking for a refund or complaining about a bad meal?
- Do you stop yourself from saying to someone that they have hurt your feelings because you don't want to hurt their feelings?
- Do you keep allowing your partner or someone else another chance when they are hurtful, disrespectful and display unacceptable behaviour?

Scores

a. If you answered 'yes' to three or more of these questions, you have some areas in your life you still need to improve on.
b. If you have answered 'yes' to six or more of these questions, you have to strengthen those courage muscles and change your perception of yourself.
c. If you answered 'yes' to more than 12 of these questions, you need to start making some changes by letting go of old limiting beliefs and negative chatter inside your head.

Why I wrote this book

Take a long, hard look at where you are with your personal and professional life, and get vigorously honest with yourself. If you are not where you want to be, what are you doing about getting there? Life isn't like a TV, you cannot press a switch and change channels. There is no remote control – you have to get up, get going and get with the programme. This book will motivate you.

When you do not have a robust inner self, you leave yourself vulnerable to disrespect, emotional and even physical abuse. Living in this fast-paced, challenging world without high self-esteem is setting yourself up for failure. I was a child model and actress from the age of 8. My agent insisted I had my legs insured in case I wrecked them if I fell over, so I was often kept home and unable to play with other children. Because of this I was bullied at school until I entered my teens. I went on to be disrespected and disregarded by boyfriends and colleagues until my early 30s. So I am not writing this book from a therapeutic point of view (although I don't wish to diminish those who do), but from real-life experience. I have enormous success with clients who have low self-esteem, lack confidence and struggle to be assertive because I can empathise with them. My approach is simple yet effective, and it works because I take a 'tough love' approach, tempered with a dose of humour and an open heart, often relating my own experiences.

The Confidence Factor is written by someone who has been where you are now, and it is easy to read. Do not be fooled by the simplicity – simplicity is the secret. This is intended to be a thought-provoking book written in an edgy and engaging style. You will find stacks of empowering strategies that are not rocket science – if you work them, I promise you they work. My life has changed beyond my wildest dreams by applying and living these principles. Peppered throughout the book are quotations to inspire you from high-profile people who overcame setbacks, including bullying, dyslexia, abuse, learning difficulties, poverty, rejections, abandonment, addictions and more. I recommend that you copy the ones that speak to you into a notebook or onto your phone and refer to them whenever you feel flat or low, to inspire you that anything is possible.

How to get the most from this book

Part 1. Getting ready to change

> 'Talk doesn't cook rice.'
>
> Chinese proverb

Changing is doing. Sure, you will get revolutionary insights from this book, but you need to get real, get going and put the seven secrets into practice to achieve tangible change. Press the pause button, and get some clarity on what your ideal life is. Buy a journal to highlight whatever leaps up at you. The whole purpose of this book is to help you learn the power of being accountable for your life, so you grow courage muscles, build a strong interior, feel more worthy, pump up your charisma and rocket your confidence. Part 1 is for you to reflect about what is working in your life and what isn't, and to encourage you to find the willingness to change.

Once you trust yourself 100% to make the right decisions for yourself, you will create the life you desire. Part 1 will shift old beliefs and blocks that are keeping you from feeling truly confident within. You may say to me, 'I know all this, I have read it so many times before'. What I would ask you is, 'Are you practising what you know?' If you are not, then you clearly haven't grasped the essence of, and the methodology for, letting go of your worn-out behaviours, thoughts and beliefs. Rituals can raise your confidence or lower your confidence. The quality of your results is a direct reflection of the quality of your mind.

It is progress, not perfection you are aiming for. It takes time, persistence and repetition to change old thoughts and old behaviours. Some clients resist changes, and you may too. Why not find a buddy and work through this book together to make yourselves more accountable? You may start off by feeling incredibly excited and enthused, then find anger bubbling up (often anger towards yourself) as you become aware of how you have allowed others to take advantage of you, or how you have procrastinated, or allowed others to put you down, or haven't listened to your intuition. If any of this happens, take a deep breath and feel free to contact me for my 12-minute mp3, which will help you to relax and let go: email me at annie@annieashdown.com.

Part 2. The seven secrets

Part 2 consists of the seven secrets. Some may leap up at you, some may not. However, they are in a sequence for a reason, so please follow them as I wrote them, strategically, so you can get the most out of the book. Every chapter consists of a secret and a variety of tips, tools and techniques. Individually, these chapters are crucial for your confidence to rocket; collectively, they are the gateway to a more empowered you. You may find you get stuck on one secret and lose interest – that's cool, no worries. Pick the book back up when you feel inclined to. But *please* do pick it up. Remember: successful people always finish what they start. As the saying has it, half-measures don't avail us half-results, half-measures avail us nothing. There is a call to action at the end of each chapter. You can skip them if you like, but remember, if you want to raise your confidence I recommend you do what successful people do and respect yourself enough to put in the hard work.

These secrets are modelled on the actions of myself and others who have learned the secrets and succeeded before you. By all means read them all straight through if you wish. However, I strongly recommend you go back and give yourself some time to process each secret so it drops from head to heart and supports you through your transition. I want you to refer to this second part of the book over and over again. These secrets must be learnt, applied and practised to bring about change. You will hear me say over and over in the book: work it, you are worth it.

A brief outline of the seven secrets

Secret 1. Self-respect

I demonstrate how successful people consider themselves important, without being egotistical. It's a fundamental aspect of confidence, as having self-respect means being comfortable with yourself.

Secret 2. Self-approval

By being kind to your mind and letting go of your harsh inner critic, you will value and trust your abilities, build resilience and start giving yourself mental hugs. Your choices and decisions will change profoundly.

Secret 3. Self-acceptance

When you accept yourself you will feel at ease being authentic. By accepting your flaws as well as your strengths you will become empowered, which will rocket your self-esteem and confidence.

Secret 4. Self-mastery

You will be shown how to gain clarity, cut through information overload and determine what works for you. By garnering self-mastery, you will discover and develop your intuitive compass, which will radically change your life.

Secret 5. Self-belief

Once you have mastered this you won't quit so easily – you will flip your weaknesses into strengths, become your own motivational coach and understand about conflicting beliefs to create a powerful you.

Secret 6. Self-accountability

Ownership and accountability are at the very heart of sustained success. I will guide you through how powerful it is to be the creator of your own life and help you stop being a victim and pointing the finger of blame at others.

Secret 7. Self-assertiveness

Once you learn the art of excellent communication skills and can make an impact with your influence and persuasion techniques, you will never want to leave home without them.

Chapter 2

DO YOU WANT THE CONFIDENCE FACTOR?

'Change will not come about if we wait for everyone else to change. We are the change that we seek.'

Barack Obama

Over the years when researching extensively and reading endless authorised biographies, studying body language and carefully observing the communication skills of high-profile, confident people, I learned that it isn't about luck but about having the right attitude, taking action, changing behaviour, taking one step, one goal, one priority at a time, a day at a time. We all have the same ability to change; what matters is how we apply ourselves. Successful people learn to have focus, discipline, motivation, awareness, intention and clarity, and after applying the seven secrets in *The Confidence Factor*, you will too.

For years I was 'Miss Nice', and yet I had so much rage inside that hadn't been dealt with. I turned that rage inwards and punished myself by starving my body or overeating. Your willpower will never be stronger than your subconscious – *never*. Everything that takes place is recorded in our subconscious, so it is vital to deal with issues head-on, to feel your feelings rather than suppressing them and paying the price. Remember: the more awareness you have, the more positive your attitude, the smarter the choices you make.

Self-confidence is the key to success in every area of your life. You have to change your consciousness to build a connection to yourself. You are not 'less than anyone else'.

Annie's quiz. Attitudes, awareness and inventory

It's time for another quiz. Again, I want you to be brutally honest with yourself as you answer each question.

- I am motivated: true or false?
- I am flexible in my approach: true or false?
- I am willing to take an informed risk: true or false?
- I am patient and compassionate, but not foolish: true or false?
- I am eager to stretch myself: true or false?
- I am positive the majority of the time: true or false?
- I am aware of my core values: true or false?
- I am willing to go to any length – so long as it's legal and moral – to make changes: true or false?
- I am out and about, looking the part without showing off: true or false?
- I am generous with sharing my expertise, skills and knowledge: true or false?
- I am quick to get back up from life's knocks: true or false?
- I am standing by my convictions with strong self-belief: true or false?
- I am my own supporter and believe in my own capabilities: true or false?
- I always champion others: true or false?
- I am uninterested in other people's opinions of me: true or false?
- I am assertive in a non-aggressive way: true or false?
- I am aware that if I don't speak my truth I am being dishonest: true or false?
- I am expert in interpersonal skills: true or false?
- I am approachable: true or false?

- I appreciate myself in a non-egotistical way: true or false?
- I am aware that I like to take care of others, as subconsciously, I want others to take care of me: true or false?
- I am aware that others often flatter me as a form of manipulation: true or false?
- I am acutely aware that being fair to others does not guarantee that they will be fair to me: true or false?

If you answered 'true' to only a few of these questions, your courage muscles are not strong. If you answered 'false' to many of these questions, your life is being driven by your old wounds and limiting beliefs. Now is the time to change. Now is the time to move from the ordinary to the extraordinary.

Do you know who you are?

'With the realisation of one's own potential and self-confidence in one's ability, one can build a better world.'

Dalai Lama

Successful people don't self-destruct, or give up in the face of adversity — they are willing to step out of their comfort zone and delve into the unknown. They are not easily diverted. The three most common traits can keep you stuck are:

1. fear of rejection
2. lack of confidence
3. limiting beliefs.

You must find the place within where you can start to believe that nothing is impossible. Don't demand and don't assume; if it is meant to be, it will happen — as they say in Scotland, 'What is for you won't go afore you.' The way you think about yourself is not always the way you actually are.

I want you to learn the importance of self-confidence and understand that when you 'build your courage muscles', you can reframe anxiety, hidden fears and current challenges. I want you to design a strategy for your life to discover your visions, dreams and goals and use effective influence, persuasion and communication skills to have an impact. And I want you to practise saying 'No' until you can say it with confidence and ease.

Are you aware of your personality?

Many psychologists follow the model of the 'big five' traits, which they believe to be the basic qualities that serve as the building blocks of personality. Personalities are complex, and you may find that you display behaviours from each of the five categories.

1. **Conscientiousness**
   - **i.** Organised
   - **ii.** Disciplined
   - **iii.** Loyal
   - **iv.** Thoughtful
   - **v.** Committed

2. **Agreeableness**
   - **i.** Affectionate
   - **ii.** Pleasant
   - **iii.** Altruistic
   - **iv.** Kind
   - **v.** Easy to be around

3. **Neuroticism**
   - **i.** Anxious
   - **ii.** Prone to depression
   - **iii.** Irritable
   - **iv.** Moody
   - **v.** Emotionally unstable

4. **Openness**
   - **i.** Adventurous
   - **ii.** Insightful

   iii. Imaginative

   iv. Creative

   v. Takes risks

5. Extraversion

   i. Assertive

   ii. Talkative

   iii. Likes to be centre of attention

   iv. Sociable

   v. Emotionally outgoing

Have you ever blown the whistle on yourself?

I want you to really get to know yourself. Stop blaming others and start identifying your own self-defeating behaviours by taking responsibility for your choices, words, thoughts, beliefs and actions. You can reframe and rewrite old scripts. Do not change your personality, which makes you unique, but let go of any unhealthy traits that demean and depreciate you.

Become your own best friend – get into self-examination to open the door to healing, growth and change. Stop feeling self-pity. Think about what it would mean to *not* make changes. Fear of success can be insidious and needs to be addressed. Why would you keep repeating the same pattern, time and time again? Any drug of choice can keep you in a constant state of inner anxiety, with a lack of confidence and low self-esteem, and you'll remain in situations where you feel trapped and unhappy.

Ready for a breakthrough?

You can't change what you do not acknowledge. You may have met many people – but now it is time to meet yourself. You will then feel comfortable standing up and declaring: 'If you find out who I really am, you may not like me. But that's your issue, not mine.'

First, discover what is sabotaging you and keeps you from taking the risks needed to make changes. Maybe you feel lonely and long for a partner, but the fear of rejection is so great on a subconscious level that you do nothing about it because it feels safer than taking the initiative. You therefore make excuses not to join a dating site, for example, or not to go out socially on the singles scene.

You have to dig deep. I can guarantee you this: somewhere within you there is a destructive pattern lurking, even if it hasn't revealed itself. Finding it and releasing it are the first steps, and then you can be aware of the areas where you need to employ more discipline. This is not about explaining or defending; this is a process of recognition. It is crucial to discover the way to self-exploration that will empower you.

Invite your shadows to tea

I use a technique in hypnotherapy that guides clients through a process to reveal the parts of themselves they struggle with. During their trance, I suggest that they invite their shadows to tea and have a group hug. I created a technique whereby clients can distinguish which shadows they are not accepting. It is very effective because it aligns all aspects of themselves, so they can accept and learn to love themselves as they are.

The parts you hide can cause problems because you hide the positive aspects as well as the negative ones. The arrogant person is forever projecting the shadows that irritate them onto others (I'll explore the crucial differences between confidence and arrogance in detail in the next chapter). However, those who lack self-confidence do the same thing. When you have confidence, you are at peace with every part of yourself. You are aware of your strengths and weaknesses and neither hide nor flaunt them, either aggressively or passively.

In 12-step programmes they often say, 'If you spot it you got it', meaning that if you can recognise someone's flaws, it's because you have them too. It is obnoxious to believe you have the right to point out the shortcomings of another. Who made it your responsibility? Are you 100% perfect?

When you commit to:

- learn a language and don't
- lose weight and don't
- change careers and don't
- quit smoking and don't

... beware it is your shadow running the show.

The psychology of successful people and unsuccessful people

Successful people:

- are aware that their net worth is not determined by power and prestige, but by their moral principles, the courage of their convictions and their sincerity
- are alert to their own needs and have the ability to see good in unexpected places and talents in unexpected people
- keep their minds free from clutter and gossip and focus on creating, not criticising
- do not focus on perfection because they know that will distract them from excellence
- are tolerant of those who make blunders, as that is how they learned
- know the difference between being productive and being busy
- do not exaggerate the sense of their own importance
- say 'I can and I will change x'
- are energised, focused and strategic
- are always open to learning
- develop and nurture a network of high achievers
- review and replenish their action plans regularly
- constantly work on improving their attitude
- expect themselves to perform to their peak

- cultivate vigorous self-honesty
- feed their mind with ongoing positive and confident thoughts
- visualise their ideal outcome
- are allergic to Negative Nancy and Negative Ned
- set and prioritise goals, take quiet time and take charge of their life.

Unsuccessful people:

- are always saying 'I wish I could change x'
- are resentful of other people's success, fame and fortune
- are big fans of procrastination and putting off making decisions
- are often moaners and self-pitying
- are rigid in their thinking
- always say 'I will try', meaning '... if I can be bothered'
- blame their 'problems' on the government, traffic, weather, the economy ... and even their cat!
- judge everyone on how they look, act, speak and think
- encourage their friends to play safe and stay small
- gossip and create drama
- hang out with Morris Moaners and Debbie Downers
- spend hours each week watching rubbish TV and reading about celebrity scandals
- bombard their minds with self-limiting beliefs and negative emotions
- focus on want, lack, trouble and difficulties
- have irrational thoughts and irrational ideas
- often sabotage opportunities
- focus on their own shortcomings
- expend time and energy discussing things that didn't work out.

THE 15 RULES OF HIGH ACHIEVERS

'People seldom do what they believe in, they do what is convenient and then repent'

Bob Dylan

High achievers:

1. take daily inventory of their stock of new, positive thoughts and beliefs and throw out the old ones like a battered old pair of shoes
2. focus on what they desire, eliminating jealousy and cynicism and committing to being accountable for all that happens
3. are aware they emulate who they associate with, so they are super-vigilant of where they place themselves
4. believe that, if they sometimes fail, they are not a failure, and if they sometimes make a mistake, they are not a mistake
5. understand about deadlines and emergencies and are respectful and reliable; however, they are captain of their own ship and don't allow others to dictate to them
6. care for their body, mind and soul
7. know when to speak up and when to stay silent
8. do not put words in other people's mouths, wanting to programme them to react predictably
9. create an inner friend, as opposed to an inner critic, and treat their inner friend with love, compassion and respect
10. don't unload their frustration, stress, fear or anger on others by dishing out inappropriate remarks or unsolicited criticism
11. are independent thinkers and refuse to engage with people who mistreat them
12. make the effort to understand others rather than to be understood

13. don't get hooked into other people's power trips or games, but maintain their dignity at all times remaining empowered and centred

14. don't presume in themselves a perfection that simply is not there

15. cast off the burdens of the past and anxieties of the future and live in the present moment.

Chapter 3
CONFIDENCE VERSUS ARROGANCE

'Confidence comes from not always being right, but not fearing being wrong.'

Sophia Loren

So many confuse arrogance for confidence. Arrogant behaviour is toxic and damaging and causes trauma and chaos, hurting others. In this chapter, I will clear up any misunderstandings you may have about confidence and arrogance. This will help you steer clear of those who are arrogant, and, because many disguise arrogance with charm, it is essential to be able to spot the difference. It is also crucial to keep the halogen light shining on your own behaviour to ensure you are developing confidence and not arrogance.

A few comparisons of arrogance and confidence

- Ignoring and denying any areas of weakness, versus accepting and admitting weaknesses.
- Pointing out someone's shortcomings – subtly or overtly – versus championing and supporting others.
- Showing off, versus possessing humility.

- Making everything about competition, versus making everything about creating value for others.
- Needing to act cool, versus being comfortable with who you are.
- Being unreasonable, versus being flexible and understanding.
- Being commanding and dominating, versus being assertive yet compassionate.
- Often being unapproachable, versus always being approachable.
- Interrupting others, versus being an effective listener.
- Swaggering when walking, versus having a commanding presence with open body language.
- Cockiness about accomplishments, versus being humble around success.
- Striving to always be right, versus striving to find a solution.
- Being constantly opinionated, versus constantly being willing to listen to others' viewpoints.
- Obsessive about image, versus taking pride in appearance.
- Never admitting mistakes, versus always being accountable to themselves.
- Positioning themselves as superior, versus viewing everyone as an equal.
- Offering unsolicited advice, versus offering feedback when it's requested.

Arrogance = Adolf Hitler

'Self-confidence must be inculcated in the young national comrade from childhood on. His whole education and training must be so ordered as to give him the conviction that he is absolutely superior to others.'

Mein Kampf, Vol. II, 1926

Confidence = Nelson Mandela

'When we let our own light shine, we unconsciously give other people permission to do the same. We ask ourselves "Who am I to be brilliant, gorgeous, talented and famous?" Who are you not to be? You are a child of God.'

Presidential inauguration speech, 5 October 1994

Hitler clearly mistook the illusion of 'absolute superiority' for self-confidence. Nelson Mandela understood that when we have confidence we value ourselves and create value for others. Big difference!

T'ien-t'ai, a sixth-century Chinese Buddhist scholar, declared those in a state of anger as 'always desiring to be superior to others', offensively displaying self-importance and superiority. He stated that anger is akin to arrogance and may be described as frustrated arrogance. The inner state of an arrogant person is constantly agitated, awaiting any opportunity to assert their sense of superiority.

The roots of arrogance

Arrogance is a deep fear of vulnerability. Many of us were persecuted as children by being made fun of at school or at home and so we grow up deeply insecure. The stereotypically arrogant person will always put others down first, thinking that, if they do, the other person won't have the opportunity to put them down. I am a recovered 'diva', so take it from me – if you recognise yourself as having arrogant traits, do something about it.

Arrogance stems from the ego, and includes a feeling of both self-contempt and contempt for others. Arrogant people feel the need to show you that they can do better than you, that they know more than you, and so many focus on competition. They have an insolent pride and overbearing manner that often upsets a lot of people. That manner stems from deep insecurity, and a lack of confidence and self-esteem. They don't value themselves and so they need to keep blowing their own trumpet. They have a sense of entitlement based on the belief that the world owes them a living and you are there for their convenience. Arrogant people just don't get that they have no right to put others down. Arrogance is unmerited confidence.

My friend Jamie says 'God save us from helpful people'. I love that! Many arrogant people firmly believe that they know what's best for you and feel that you are not bright enough to figure it out for yourself, insisting on giving unsolicited advice.

Many arrogant people display a type of shyness, because they feel that if they hide away no-one will see their flaws, so they won't be judged or criticised. However, the arrogant person will always jump in with unfair and inaccurate criticism of other people. The confident person will have a sense of proportion, will be respectful and fair, and will have a sense of compassion and respect when offering feedback. All arrogant people (even the shy ones) are judgemental.

Sam Roddick – Exercising humility

Sam Roddick displays such humility. In common with her mother – the legendary Dame Anita Roddick – she is devoid of all arrogance.

Sam opened two shops in London and one in Los Angeles, where Brad Pitt and Angelina Jolie are regular customers. She didn't allow being dyslexic to hold her back; in fact, she turned it into a positive trait, crediting it for her ability to listen and remember. She left school at 16 with two O levels.

Sam told me:

My parents and grandmother have an incredible amount of bravery and integrity. They speak the truth and don't dress life's bullshit. They are down to earth, kind and very funny and human, and humility comes above everything they do. Life is not about what you achieve but enjoying the process. When I was young, other people's opinions used to eat me up — both positive and negative. I hated it when people used to compliment me because I would feel like a fraud, and when people were negative I believed everything they said was true — I feel like people's negative opinion can be like a contagious disease in the soul. But now I am older I am interested and curious but almost unattached to people's opinions — I find the negative equally informative as the positive; there is always a hidden seed of truth in both. To me, now, truth is almost irrelevant: what is interesting is perception and what I can learn from it, how I can grow. Sometimes criticism is the best form of growth you can get — equally, compliments can quench the spirit. My motivation is my imagination and the belief that the goodness inside each one of us can be reached to perform great and simple, small and profound acts of humanity — I want to inspire a sense of empowerment and belief that the world can be a better, kinder, more loving place and all we need to do is imagine it and then act on it.

Sam's top tips. *Don't worry about looking like a fool. When you have the humility to ask questions you display a lack of arrogance and instead demonstrate self-confidence and a hunger to learn.*

Annie's thoughts. *Sam displays all the traits of a confident person by not caring what others think, and not worrying if she makes mistakes. She favours profound acts of humanity, which you would never catch an arrogant person doing. It isn't in their nature to inspire and to be kind.*

Arrogance is a turn-off, confidence is a turn-on

An arrogant person is characterised by thinking, 'I am right, you are wrong'. In fact, 'you' statements often suggest arrogance, as it's presumptuous to imagine you know how others feel or think and to dictate what the issue and solution are.

Successful people communicate in a way that is inoffensive. Arrogant people have an inflated view of their own self-worth and when tackling them they often respond in a hostile and aggressive manner.

Arrogant people are unable to participate in honest, spirited debates and conversations without showing disrespect and even contempt. Arrogance doesn't want us to have any flaws. Confident people possess 'HOW' – honesty, openness and willingness – keys to growth and change. Arrogant people have blind spots, so they don't see their own shortcomings, but they love spotting yours. They see others as objects they can control, manipulate, ignore or use as and when they want.

> 'It is rare to find nice loyal people you can trust in the music and TV business. They are diamonds. When I started out, many tried to make it difficult and were very negative. With me, loyalty and honesty is everything and if someone breaks that then I have a problem.'
>
> Simon Cowell, speaking to Jim Naughtie on BBC Radio 4, May 2012

Arrogant people are not loyal or honest; they are out for number one, at all costs. Those with self-confidence are loyal and can be trusted. If confident people make mistakes or misjudge something or someone, they re-evaluate and self-examine and see the facts without making too much of a big deal about it, then they take on the responsibility to change. It's completely futile to ask anyone who is arrogant to examine what lies behind their huge defence mechanism, as all they do is turn it back on you. They project onto others what they deny within themselves, never see you as an equal, and are irrational. Many are intellectual and therefore have little time for emotion.

Finally, society is starting to catch on and is not allowing so many rewards to accrue to the arrogant. In the US, many TV producers now go through the public's Twitter remarks about each character on a show. The public is starting to be drawn towards authenticity, and therefore characters are often written out of a show if the public feel they are disingenuous.

As Nicole Scherzinger quite rightly said on *The X Factor* in 2012: 'It's crucial to know the difference between cockiness and confidence.'

Ambiguity frightens arrogant people because it suggests imperfection, change and lack of certainty. They have to control everyone and everything, and, although many achieve success through charm or by inheriting substantial wealth, they often reach the top of the ladder to find they have few friends – and the friends they do have are as unreliable, untrustworthy and arrogant as themselves. Many come unstuck after years of seemingly having it all. Many have success and recognition for a period of time and then lose it. Others maintain their success but it doesn't bring them rich friendships, rich experiences, inner peace or joy. For many it brings untreated addictions, bankruptcy, divorce, scandals, isolation and pain.

Arrogant people have a false charm, and many people don't see through this, but the arrogant also have no problem revealing their cruel side to those they don't like. The more they don't like someone, the bigger the threat and the harsher the criticism.

Flattery and battery

It's important for me to add that sometimes people who dominate the conversation are nervous and not necessarily arrogant. Also, people might drop names to impress you because they feel insecure; it isn't always because they are arrogant. The way to spot the difference is to look at whether they possess empathy or compassion, which only confident people possess.

It is always helpful to learn skills to deal with arrogance because there is a lot of it about and we can't always avoid it. But in a social setting

I recommend you stay well away, as arrogant people can cause pain, especially if you get involved with them romantically. Be aware: if you question arrogant people they will react badly – don't take their reaction personally, though, as it's about their inability to control you.

So many people who lack confidence want to hang out with 'cool', arrogant people who are famous, extremely rich or good-looking and who generally use fake charm (which evaporates if you anger them). Sadly, the people who agree with their every word, flattering them and putting them on a pedestal, are not achieving anything great in their own lives and are living vicariously through the other person.

Arrogant people will get into character assassination behind your back, joke about people they really shouldn't joke about, and lack empathy if someone is going through a hard time even though they may pretend to care. They themselves have been hurt badly in their past and, instead of resolving or addressing the issue, they hide it behind a mask. They generally won't mock anyone going through a difficult time in public, as they are concerned about their own image and want to be seen as perfect and charming, but they judge, knock and mock anyone who they feel is too passive to hit back. If they are rumbled, they deliver those old classic lines: 'I was only joking', or 'Stop being so sensitive.'

> 'When you don't feel confident about yourself, you look for flaws in others to make yourself feel better. The hardest thing is to free yourself from caring what someone says about you.'
>
> Tina Fey

Arrogant people genuinely believe they are intrinsically better than everyone else and have a lack of appreciation of anyone else's talents and gifts. It amazes me when someone who can't sing to save their life or has never taken a risk criticises performers on *The X Factor*. They think it's clever to be offensive and they generally have little insight because they are so wrapped up in themselves. The truth is that they like to control everyone, which is a form of emotional abuse. If you have experienced this controlling behaviour when you were young, you won't spot it easily because it will be familiar and, in a perverse way, comfortable, because it is what you are used to. Many egotistical people make themselves appear charming, and many are clever with words. I constantly hear clients, colleagues and friends seduced and hooked, oblivious to the fact that these charming people can be dangerous and are using subtle ways to control and manipulate them.

Arrogant people speak over you, at you or down to you. They insist that you listen to them but rarely, if ever, listen to you, even though they may pretend to. They generalise from their limited, narrow life experiences and impose their small world view on others. They believe that being assertive means attempting to validate themselves in the eyes of others. This is why so many arrogant people genuinely believe that they are confident.

Meet **Stephen** – who moved from Arrogance City to Confidence City.

I joined a city law firm as a graduate and believed I knew more than the senior partners, ignoring the tips and advice I was offered. I alienated many of my colleagues with my behaviour. I had been told as a child I was better than everyone, as they thought that was instilling confidence in me. I couldn't see my shortcomings or admit to any mistakes, which was where the problem lay. Five years on, I now see how being arrogant cost me so much, both personally and professionally. I am now a partner in a law firm; and, having spent five years investing in self-development and taking my own inventory to develop self-awareness, I now cringe when I see others play out my old behaviour. It's been a painful yet eye-opening learning curve, but since working with Annie and applying her suggestions, techniques and tools, I have radically changed and my confidence has risen immensely. Thanks to Annie being brutally honest and helping me discover my blind spots.

Stephen's top tips. *Stop measuring your own value by externals. Let go of the need to be right and to always have the last word. Admit your own shortcomings to yourself and let go of the need to act superior, which is a real turn-off.*

Annie's thoughts. *Stephen was full of self-doubt, which is the most crippling limitation you can face in life. Now he has found self-confidence (a strong belief in his own judgement), he knows he will succeed and doesn't feel threatened by others, or concerned about what they feel about him.*

My story

I mistook my arrogance for confidence. I achieved success by blagging my way through with an air of fake confidence. On the outside I acted superior to everyone else, yet on the inside, I felt inferior. I was conscious of my weight as I went from having less fat on me than a chip to looking like a sumo wrestler. I also suffered from chronic depression, insomnia and had tantrums when I didn't get my own way. When success came, I found a subtle way to sabotage it. When my father offered solid, caring, practical advice, I rebelled because I thought I knew best.

I had a severe meltdown in 2000 when my eating disorder spun out of control. Change comes from desperation or inspiration, and it was the former that sparked my journey of self-discovery.

I had to heal the wounds of my past. I could no longer sit in Self-Pity City pointing the finger of blame at everyone else. I tried a vast mix of conventional and complementary therapies on a one-to-one basis, each costing £100 an hour and ending in 'y'. I also explored Buddhism, shamanism, chanting and Kabbalah. I spent a fortune on various different seminars, retreats and workshops. In fact, I found many of these principles and techniques to be very effective and incorporate them in my practice today.

I learned a lot about myself and I healed a lot of wounds. After working through my own difficulties, my ego was smashed and my arrogance shrank. I hired a life coach, a hypnotherapist, an emotional freedom technique (EFT) practitioner and a healer. Recognising the tangible benefits they brought about, I changed my direction from training as a psychologist to training as a coach, hypnotherapist, EFT practitioner and healer so that I could help others move forward.

Before finding my inner confidence and self-respect, I allowed myself to be blown about by every wind. If someone praised me I felt good; if someone put me down I felt bad. I was like a puppet on a string, pulled and pushed every which way by external forces and opinions. My inner core was so weak and damaged that I had to strengthen it the same way we work a muscle in the gym, to become strong. I had to be persistent and disciplined, with daily practice, to make changes.

If I can change after years of severe bullying, a chronic eating disorder, people-pleasing, low self-esteem and a lack of confidence, and start standing up for myself in a non-aggressive way, build confidence and self-esteem and fulfil my visions, dreams and goals, so can you. The seven secrets work: don't take my word for it, give them a go!

I urge you to recognise signs of arrogance in yourself and others. If it's in yourself, it is time to stop ignoring it. If it is with others, it is time to come out of denial about them and see through their disguise. Your arrogance can wreck friendships, business partnerships, love, romance and work relationships, and others' arrogance can harm you, professionally or personally.

Are you arrogant or confident?

When you find yourself condemning others, check whether or not the issue is important enough to invest time and energy in it. Are you doing it to position yourself as better than them?

How good are you at:

- resolving conflict?
- negotiating?
- identifying others' needs?

- confronting issues?
- considering others' feelings?

'Too many people spend money they haven't earned to buy things they don't want to impress people they don't like.'

Will Smith

Uncovering the essence of confidence

The *Tao Te Ching* says:

> To understand others is to have knowledge;
> To understand oneself is to be illuminated,
> To conquer others needs strength;
> To conquer oneself is harder still.
> To be content with what one has is to be rich ...

Confident people are rich as they have self-belief, open hearts and treat others with respect, honour other people's boundaries and inspire, motivate and champion others.

Confident people are sensitive and respectful to others' emotions as they are in touch with their own. They are kind and generous in spirit and interested in others. Confident people have a greater life experience as they are open-minded. They are the type of people you love. Confident people are those you love being around and those who may be the boss of the company but are happy to give you a lift home or make the tea if necessary.

Confident people accept themselves so they accept others as they find them, yet arrogant people have a hard time tolerating anyone who is different to them, and have an enormous inability to see anyone else's point of view. They speak harshly and cruelly about people they don't like (which is most people).

Confident employers love having confident people working for them, and people love being around confident people socially as they are so comfortable with themselves. Even an enemy or competitor secretly admires a self-confident person. In the workforce, the confident leader is aware of the team's needs, the client's needs and changes in the working environment and the economy. In a relationship, the confident partner is aware of what needs to be discussed and communicates changes in a healthy way.

'I had to tune out what the hell everybody else had to say about who I was. When I was able to do that, I felt free.'

Queen Latifah

SUMMARY. EVALUATING AND ENDORSING

◆ I suggest you develop a checklist to determine any shortcomings you may have, such as that shown below. By compiling an inventory you will heighten your awareness, help you correct your ineffective behaviour and evaluate whether you are acting arrogantly.

◆ Focus on clear intentions so you can contribute daily to your commitment to change.

◆ Are you willing to take on new challenges, or are you reluctant?

◆ Make a list of qualities you admire in others.

◆ Are you focused on fixing yourself rather than fixing others?

◆ Keep your new tools with you when you are around arrogant people. Do not allow them to seduce you.

◆ Exercise humility and keep checking that you are acting confidently, not arrogantly.

A call to action

1. The lessons I have learned about arrogance versus
confidence are:

....
....

2. A person or situation I have needed confidence around is:

....
....

3. I have been fearful because:

....
....

4. The excuses I might make to avoid facing this fear are:

....
....

5. The steps I will take to overcome my fears and build my
confidence are:

....
....

ANNIE'S CONFIDENCE-BOOSTERS

- ◆ Get comfortable with showing up but not showing off.
- ◆ Constantly set new written goals.
- ◆ Remain humble and sincere.
- ◆ Talk less, listen more.
- ◆ Have belief in your own decision-making.

Chapter 4

FLEX THOSE COURAGE MUSCLES AND LEARN TO CHANGE

'Anything is possible if you have enough nerve.'

J. K. Rowling

I urge you to go beyond your comfort zone and summon up the courage to change. Own your power, be what you want to be, do what you want to do, have what you want to have. Self-awareness, self-knowledge and self-investigation are all prerequisites for change, but first you need an open heart and an open mind. Transformation depends entirely on your conscious choices, your heightened awareness and your willingness to stand back from yourself and observe your thoughts, beliefs and reactions to others before taking action.

Behavioural scientists and evidence-based clinicians are increasingly suggesting that building self-confidence helps to make and sustain lasting changes in our behaviours. Successful people create a winning strategy. They set the stage, organise the lighting, hire the crew and direct the play. You need to focus not so much on what needs changing in the world, and what others need to change in themselves, but on what beliefs, thoughts and attitudes *you* need to change.

You have to set boundaries, but remain flexible. You may understand the importance of logic, but the world is not always logical. Successful people are not interested in who is right and who is wrong. They are interested in changing what isn't working. They are courageous and bold – they do not understand the word 'no' and you never catch them saying 'yeah, but ...'

This chapter will demonstrate how powerful it is to know your personality and observe when you react and why you were triggered. You can only reap what you sow. One of the biggest challenges many of us have is our resistance to change. If you look for stability everywhere and for everything to remain the same, you will never find the courage to change.

'The price of doing the same old thing is far higher than the price of change.'

Bill Clinton

Annie's quiz. How courageous are you?

As with the previous quizzes, please answer based on how you feel today, not how you feel things ought to be. Please tick the statements that apply to you, regardless of the frequency (sometimes or often).

- ☐ I say yes to things I don't want to do.
- ☐ I diminish myself by putting myself down.
- ☐ I allow others to put me down in a jokey and non-jokey way.
- ☐ I worry about what others think of me.
- ☐ I settle for less by having low expectations.
- ☐ I allow fear to stop me from achieving my goals.
- ☐ I struggle to say 'No' without justifying my reasons.
- ☐ I ignore my intuition and do what others suggest.
- ☐ I feel guilty when I haven't done anything wrong.
- ☐ I compare and despair.
- ☐ I feel anxious most of the time.

- ☐ I focus on the negative.
- ☐ I have a reluctance to put myself first.
- ☐ I struggle to accept compliments.
- ☐ I feel more comfortable giving than receiving.
- ☐ I feel I have a lack of social skills.
- ☐ I fail to recognise the full potential of my abilities.
- ☐ I struggle to reveal my innermost thoughts.
- ☐ I have unrealistic expectations of perfection.
- ☐ I have a fear of change.
- ☐ I don't like making mistakes.
- ☐ I have a habit of idolising others.
- ☐ I feel inferior to others.
- ☐ I justify and defend my actions.
- ☐ I become defensive or defiant when criticised.
- ☐ I shower someone with compliments to win them over.
- ☐ I constantly beat myself up.
- ☐ I feel inadequate and incompetent.
- ☐ I have an inability to discern who and when to trust.
- ☐ I tend to remain in partnerships that are unsatisfying or abusive.
- ☐ I have firm opinions.
- ☐ I judge others who think differently to me.
- ☐ I doubt my ability to make good decisions.
- ☐ I take things personally and am very sensitive.
- ☐ I tend to attribute my success to luck.
- ☐ I have no idea what pleases me as I am too busy pleasing others.
- ☐ I feel insecure and I need my family's or friends' approval.
- ☐ I attract toxic people.
- ☐ I don't feel I deserve success.
- ☐ I worry when others don't like me.
- ☐ I don't go for promotion.
- ☐ I feel I must always be a follower, rather than a leader.
- ☐ I feel furious with myself if I make a mistake.

☐ I struggle to take criticism from others, even when constructive.
☐ I fear confrontation.
☐ I bottle up my anger, then feel resentful.
☐ I find it hard to let go of toxic people.
☐ I feel miserable not being in a relationship.
☐ I quit when things don't go my way.

Scores

35 or more ticks

You have chronic low self-confidence and no self-belief. You focus on what's going wrong and what you haven't achieved, rather than looking at what you have achieved and feeling gratitude. You look for constant approval and need everyone to think of you as nice, so you struggle to say 'no'.

20–34 ticks

You lack self-confidence and, although you are beginning to recognise your skills, you are very self-critical. This will stop you from achieving excellence, as you are far too focused on perfection. You often compare and despair. You struggle to ask for help and are uncomfortable expressing yourself directly and honestly without defending and justifying yourself.

10–19 ticks

Although you have a certain amount of confidence, you may also be confusing it with ego and arrogance. Have a good look at yourself – do you like to impose your opinions on others? Do you feel the need to have the last word and prove your point? Do you think you're better looking or more intelligent than other people? Ask yourself why you judge and criticise anyone who has more wealth or success than you.

Annie's four vital keys to being courageous

1. Pulling on your boots of self-awareness
2. Keeping the halogen light on your behaviour
3. Stop reacting and take action
4. Making smarter choices

Key 1. Pulling on your boots of self-awareness

Get to know your feelings, thoughts, behaviours and actions. They belong to you and you act them out. Self-awareness is the prerequisite for change. Become empowered by stepping back from your busy schedule and reflecting about who you are and what your strengths and weaknesses are. Bad habits keep you imprisoned, so you have to monitor your feelings and behaviour as they are the key to self-regulation. Remember: unconscious choices are reactions; conscious choices are responses. Teenagers react. If you are an adult, act like an adult, not a teenager.

When you pull on the boots of self-awareness, you find out your personality traits, personal values, habits, emotions and psychological needs that drive your behaviours. Without being aware of these, how can you change them? Do you feel worthy or unworthy, grateful or ungrateful, motivated or lethargic, secure or insecure, content or discontent, rushed or calm, unfit or fit, happy or unhappy, lovable or unlovable, deserving or undeserving, comfortable or uncomfortable? Are you aware of how you feel?

Take control of your life, set boundaries and understand your values, to ensure that you act with integrity. How can you excel as a leader at work or improve your life if you don't know yourself well? How can you have a solid relationship with others if you don't have a solid relationship with yourself?

Key 2. Keeping the halogen light on your behaviour

Others may get irritated if things don't work out, and blame you or verbally attack you. Unless you keep shining the light on your behaviour, chances are that you will be seduced, tricked and manipulated into doing what pleases others. You may feel angry inside, angry at yourself, but if you are in denial and not in touch with your feelings, or your behaviour, you can't see it. Until you take full responsibility, stay aware of what works for you and what doesn't and act accordingly, until you can keep doing what is best for you and what feels right for you, you cannot increase your confidence.

Focus on one behaviour at a time, otherwise you will be overwhelmed – you might quit and revert to your old ways. You need to commit to the changes you make. Be tenacious, keep focused on your goal. Do not be swayed by distractions or wrapped up in complaining about others' behaviour. You need to learn about you.

Ask for feedback and don't be a martyr. Don't struggle to find your way in the dark if you have access to a lamp and can lean over and switch it on. Ask trusted friends if they can see anything in you that maybe you can't see in yourself. Every time something triggers strong reactions in you, check your emotions and thoughts to see whether they are supporting you or encumbering you.

While you are discovering yourself, be gentle. Observe yourself daily without judgement (I will demonstrate a simple technique for this later). You are who you are, and everything you have done to this point has been with the knowledge and skills you have had at any given moment. Had you known differently back then, you would have behaved differently. No-one is without insecurity, fears and faults, but confident people learn to make peace with these parts of themselves, because all behaviours are connected to inner beliefs (which we will cover throughout the book).

Key 3. Stop reacting and take action

Be completely honest with yourself. Change requires self-motivation: are you clear about what you want to change and what you don't want to change? What will happen if you do change and what will happen if you don't? There is a difference between choosing not to do something and choosing to do nothing. Wanting to change your life is not enough. Fear is the force that keeps you stuck. Are you talking about what you want but not taking action? Each of us created our present situation by the choices we made in the past. Courage is the key.

We cannot expect things to change if we are scared of uncertainty. Successful people do not ask others to do what they are not willing to do themselves. Would you go onto a motorway and swerve all over the place? Successful people do not swerve all over the place: they align their behaviours with what they want to achieve, they stay on course and keep their focus where it belongs. They don't have tantrums if things go wrong or point the finger of blame at someone or something else.

They take informed risks. They take advice, yet make their own decisions. They are relentlessly driven in pursuit of their goals and overcome any fears by having faith in the unknown. So, rather than lying on the sofa, planning, analysing, worrying and going around in circles, get proactive, get productive, make a choice and just do it.

The only way to banish fear is to walk through it. Don't tell me it is all about luck. I don't buy into that. I believe that fear has become all too easy to use as an excuse these days. Many people will try to persuade you to stay small because they lack confidence and feel uncomfortable when you want to take a leap of faith, and so they transfer their fear onto you. Do *not* listen to these people.

Be aware that when you try to hide your weaknesses through fear, they will become more powerful and more visible.

Key 4. Making smarter choices

What has happened in the past has happened. Why would you want to waste time and energy discussing and analysing what happened way back that you cannot change? Negative thoughts and emotions have no place in your life.

When you are your own person and love yourself, you are not caught up in negative thinking, you begin to have more self-worth, to improve your relationships with others and to trust yourself more. You also become strategic in the way you make decisions.

It's crucial to remember that you make your own choices. Successful people make decisions and don't hesitate. Each choice you make takes you down a different road and teaches you something new, and the immediate results are either positive or negative. Successful people choose to have positive habits when it comes to decision-making. Often they enlist an expert or do their own research before making a choice, but then they use their intuition to make that choice. If it's the wrong choice, they learn from it and don't repeat it.

If you are controlled or limited by fear, you will never make a decision. You need to ask the right questions, and not moan or blame others. It's not about you being wealthier or thinner or more resourceful, it's about you maximising your potential. Don't put things on hold; don't delay happiness or success. Be clear about what you want, have faith that you will make the right choices for yourself, ask for help if you need it, then make your own decisions.

'It is our choices that show what we truly are, far more than our abilities.'

J. K. Rowling

I find **Judy Piatkus** courageous. Judy is the founder of Piatkus Books, which she started from her bedroom 30 years ago; she has since became one of the most successful independent publishers in the world. Judy was described by *The Times* as 'one of the world's leading thinkers'.

Judy told me:

I am always inspired by brave people as it's hard to be courageous. What really keeps me motivated and taking courageous steps is wanting to leave the world a better place, even if only in the tiniest of ways, and in the old days if you had asked me the key to success I would have said perseverance. But I have changed my mind and now feel it is focus — the ability to stay focused on what I want to achieve. Saying that, when things haven't worked out, I have always picked myself up and tried again, when appropriate. I admire loving people, those who are kind, generous and have the courage to be outspoken at the right time.

Judy's top tips. *Never worry about what others think of you. Their attitude to you is never about you; it is always about them. Have the courage to go for it.*

Annie's thoughts. *Judy, like other successful people, strives for a bigger purpose and by doing so she grows her courage muscles and inspires others to be courageous.*

Excuse me, what's your excuse?

Coco Chanel's mother died when she was 12 years old and her father abandoned her. She grew up in an orphanage. Yet she established herself as the 20th century's single most important arbiter of fashion. It is widely documented that, on her death in 1971, the Chanel empire was bringing in over $160 million a year. Luck? I think not.

In 1973, Jothy Rosenberg had his leg amputated above the knee because of osteosarcoma. In 1976, the cancer metastasised and two-fifths of his lungs had to be removed. He went on to get a PhD in computer science, wrote two technical books, founded six companies, rode in the Pan-Massachusetts bike-a-thon, swam from Alcatraz to San

Francisco, and has participated in many more fund-raising activities. Excuses? I think not!

Successful people are courageous, determined, motivated and disciplined. For many, these are learned behaviours. I am not interested in you moaning that you didn't get the one job this year you applied for and so you are quitting. Successful people persevere and stand by their convictions with unswerving passion. Many moguls, tycoons, athletes, movie stars, entrepreneurs and inventors achieved greatness through their invincible spirit. Sure, they have their faults and weaknesses – they're human – but they don't let these get in their way: they flex their courage muscles.

> 'I had to start at the bottom and climb very slowly to whatever you perceive to be the top. I am glad I did it that way. I wouldn't have wanted any quick breaks.'
>
> Simon Cowell

Simon Cowell left school with two O levels, joined EMI in 1979 in the post room, and worked his way up to producer. Five years later he set up a company called Fanfare Records with Iain Burton. In 1989, Fanfare's mother company folded and drove the business into bankruptcy, leaving Simon in severe debt and with no choice but to move back to his parents'. In 2006, Simon signed up as a judge on *American Idol* (earning him $20 million per series) and made a deal with Fox allowing his production company, Syco, to broadcast *Britain's Got Talent*. In the UK, he signed a multimillion pound 'golden handcuffs' deal that gave ITV the rights to *The X Factor*.

Who says degrees are the only way forward?

I could have listed many highly successful, and very different, people with no degree, no experience in their chosen field, no hand-outs from rich parents. However, I chose these three as their stories inspire me.

- **Ellen DeGeneres** is one of America's most loved TV hosts and has won 13 Emmy awards. According to *Forbes*, she was worth $53 million in 2012. She didn't go to college.
- **Bill Gates**, chairman of Microsoft, dropped out of Harvard University to concentrate on software development. According to *Forbes*, he had a net worth of $40 billion in 2009.
- **Andreas Panayiotou** is in his mid–40s and is the son of Cypriot immigrants. He is dyslexic and cannot read. He grew up in the East End of London, left school with no qualifications, and is now ranked at 200 on *The Sunday Times* Rich List with an estimated worth of over £500 million.

So I tend to switch off when I hear any of the following excuses.

- I don't have a degree.
- I am too old.
- I am not experienced in that.
- My family and friends won't approve.
- I have already lost one business.
- I don't want to marry again as it went wrong before.
- I don't have the time.
- I don't have any money.
- I have children.
- I may fail.

Stop telling everyone why you cannot do something. It is a waste of energy. Focus on what you *can* do. Excuses are so last season. Excuses always ensure defeat, so they are a bad habit to fall into.

'Even if you don't have the confidence, you have to get out there and act as if you do.'

Ashton Kutcher

Are you ready for transformation?

Are you willing to see things from another perspective? Do you feel inspired to respect yourself, to believe in yourself and feel confident enough to be authentic? Nowadays, many seek social acceptance and belonging to feel successful and worthy. Are you ready for transformation?

'The only failure is not to ever try.'

George Clooney

Making it happen

If what you are doing isn't working, why would you want to continue to do it? I am passionate about everything I have written, and there are no tools or tips I haven't used and don't continue to use myself. I have travelled the path you are on, and I continue to work on my own self-mastery. These seven secrets are not a short-cut to mental, spiritual and emotional sobriety, but applying them will help you break the cycle of what isn't working.

You have to want to make changes, then you will feel it's worth investing your time and energy in making them. Ask yourself – do you neglect your goals because you are too busy responding to the needs and wants of your partner, colleagues, children, parents and siblings?

Be honest and take an objective inventory of your own behaviour

Do you feel confident enough to allow others to identify their own problems, rather than trying to fix them yourself because of your need to be needed? Can you step back and support them rather than taking over, believing you have all the answers to everyone else's problems, and telling them that they aren't smart enough to figure it out themselves?

I shared a stage with **Maria Kempinksa** MBE, founder of Jongleurs Comedy Club, and found her so courageous. Maria opened her first club at the age of 28 with no business plan, no knowledge of business and no savings. She had passion, a £300 overdraft and a determination to succeed. Jongleurs helped launch the careers of Jack Dee, Paul Merton, Hugh Laurie, Stephen Fry, Eddie Izzard and Graham Norton, to name but a few. Fifteen years later, Maria sold the company in a deal that valued it at £30 million.

Maria told me:

My parents were my inspiration. They had to work extremely hard as they were political refugees and had to make their lives in a new country. They taught me that you can get through anything and make something new happen. I am also inspired by Richard Branson as I find him a diverse visionary and very intelligent. Linda Bennett, who founded L. K. Bennett, also inspires me as she is so creative, caring and unassumingly brilliant. My motivation for my business has always been to create value for others by putting on a brilliant Jongleurs show with everyone around you laughing and then hearing the audience say they had a brilliant time — that's a great motivator. The best piece of advice anyone ever gave me was 'find a way to make it happen'. I have suffered my own rejections, like everyone else, and although at times I found it difficult, it doesn't stop me from achieving my goal. I really admire those who have discipline, multi-layered thinking, honesty and determination, and who make creativity real.

Maria's top tips. *You can make anything happen with sheer determination, hard work, courage and discipline. When suffering rejections, pick yourself straight back up and start again.*

Annie's thoughts. *Maria had virtually nothing when she started in terms of financial support or knowledge of the industry, but she had the courage to 'make it happen'.*

Follow the crowd or stand out

'If you are lucky enough to be different from everyone else, don't change.'

Taylor Swift

Those of you who go with the flow become victims of circumstance, as you are avoiding making decisions. If that's you, it's hardly surprising that nothing changes. Some of you may choose wishful thinking over taking action, but how will that improve your life? It won't. You have to consider your options, then make decisions.

So many people are afraid of failing or of others' opinions and do nothing. Taking action, learning, then adjusting is how you reach your goals. Every time you make an effort to change, something changes. Whatever the outcome, the change will increase your knowledge and strengthen your confidence muscles, and you will learn what works and what doesn't. This process increases your skills so you can then make smarter choices. Do not wait to feel worthy of making changes, just make them now, one small step at a time to build your worthiness.

Only you can decide whether you are willing or not, and these changes have to be non-negotiable – when you make a promise to yourself, you have to stick by it, otherwise you will find old habits creeping in and you will slip backwards after the initial enthusiasm wears off. If you are consistent when making a commitment to help others, you must do the same for yourself.

The Dalai Lama was asked to describe in one word the secret to living a healthy life. His answer? 'Routines.'

Rituals and routines help you achieve consistency and balance in your life, which are essential if you're going to stick with the commitments you've made to yourself.

Fire your committee

When you are introduced to new concepts, your mind will resist and look for ways you can fail before you can even think about changing.

Many of us have to get rid of the negative 'committee' in our head. It isn't us – it's a team of 'committee members' we have picked up over the years.

Often they sit at the foot of your bed, eagerly waiting for you to wake up so they can pounce on you. They love to make you anxious (which, as you know, is futile and doesn't change anything); it's simply an attempt by our committee to control our future by making us think:

- I will never get that promotion
- she will never agree to go on a date
- I will never be as smart as my brother
- I won't pass that exam
- he won't give me a raise
- I am not strong enough to run my own business
- I can't walk out of this relationship
- I will never be able to learn French
- I won't lose weight.

This constant noise from our committee can keep us awake, can feed us lies, destroy our self-confidence and self-esteem and cause havoc. It's highly dysfunctional, highly exhausting, highly boring and highly destructive. It talks down to you, keeps you small and mocks you. It is greedy: it wants to rob you of everything – self-respect, dignity and happiness.

Stop allowing it to control your life. Your committee will lie to you and do anything to keep you from changing. You need to have a daily strategy and immediately replace the negative with a positive, as the more you fire those neurons, the stronger the pattern becomes. Your committee will rattle on, 24/7, to get your attention on a subconscious and conscious level. It can challenge your strongest beliefs about yourself.

'I am learning how to drown out the constant noise that is such an inseparable part of my life. I don't have to prove anything to anyone, I only have to follow my heart and concentrate on what I want to say to the world. I run my world.'

Beyoncé

Being confident means being yourself and mastering the art of authenticity, displaying a uniqueness that makes you influential, unforgettable and humble.

Research shows that much of what you think of as being down to genetics is in fact learned behaviour. Stop saying 'Others are lucky', or 'It's OK for them'. They broke the cycle of old habits and stopped doing things that were not working. They don't worry about what you think of them.

When you lack confidence you get your feelings of self-worth and self-esteem from being liked by others, and you invest a lot of time and energy doing and saying things you think will make others like you. I won awards for needing to be liked, and it was exhausting.

The more you look for approval, the less you get; the less you look for it, the more you get.

Do you minimise, alter, deny, justify or ignore your feelings and focus on other people's? If so, it is because you don't feel worthy of being loved or respected, so you settle for needing to be needed, hoping you will make yourself so indispensable that bosses won't fire you and partners won't leave you. Often, you become jealous of others' success. Many people with low self-confidence need to be seen as nice at all costs, yet often are full of resentment as their sensitivity to rejection is so high they avoid risks at all costs.

You are perfectly imperfect

If you suffer with low self-confidence, you will feel more comfortable around drama, chaos and crisis; when things are going well, you will feel out of sorts. I used to get so cross with anyone moaning when we were out – it got in the way of my own moaning. I was a chameleon, changing my views and values to match everyone else's. I didn't know what my values, opinions or needs were, as I had spent so long focusing on everyone else's.

Aiming to be perfect means you set unrealistically high goals and put enormous pressure on yourself to reach them. If you don't achieve them you may feel some shame, which will create a lot of discomfort within and could result in you wanting to give up.

> 'I think imperfections are important, just as mistakes are important. You only get to be good by making mistakes. You only get to be real by being imperfect.'
>
> Julianne Moore

Do you soak up everyone else's emotions and feel responsible when things go wrong in other people's lives, believing you need to fix them even though you didn't break them? Are you aware that this is another way to delay making changes and creating your own success?

Negative habits are taught to us or we pick them up along the way. They are not inherited as part of your biological make-up, so you have the power within you to change them.

Having low self-confidence means you have no trust in yourself, and this inhibits your ability to take a risk, speak up, be assertive and dare to live your dreams.

The idealised self

The 'idealised self' is one you feel you should be like to be acceptable. The term 'shadow' was first used by Carl Jung to describe the repressed part of the self. Often, we learn that certain aspects of ourselves are unacceptable to others as we grow up. The paradox is that when you accept and embrace your shadow, you find hidden gold. I always explain to clients that I am not giving them confidence, I am like a diver going in search of their gold. They have all the assets they need but their assets are undiscovered within.

'Should' and 'try' are words we often use subconsciously. When you use these words, ask yourself – is this me speaking, or my shadow? If your shadow is speaking, the words will have the following, negative meanings.

Should = I think I have to do x, y or z but I don't really want to.

Try = I know x, y or z needs to be done, but I don't really care if it gets done or if it doesn't.

Perhaps you were shamed as a child for crying or punished for displaying anger or told you were showing off when you were proud of an achievement? If so, it may cause you to repress those parts of yourself that caused you pain. Perhaps you thought of them as being bad, so you hid them and they became your shadows.

Own every aspect of yourself

When you repress your anger so you can be the nice person, always doing as you are told, you are in desperate need of others' approval. Do you believe that if you are nice, others will be nice to you? That is rarely the case, and sometimes it's the opposite. You need to develop courage muscles to be yourself and learn how to deal with anger in a healthy way by turning it into assertiveness.

If you fear getting in touch with your repressed anger or sadness, go to see a therapist. It is always better out than in. I had chronic depression for 20 years off and on, but I no longer have it because I dealt with my anger, which was suppressed and made me depressed. Your shadow wields enormous power over your life.

Your shadow predicts your behaviours and controls how much success you are entitled to and how much failure you experience. When you try to be someone else and don't accept your shadow self, you often sabotage success and goals. It can take a while to get there, as your shadow has its own agenda, at odds with your conscious self.

'A magical thing happened when I turned 40 — a light sort of went off, and I felt more self-assured and self-confident. It was like I finally had the right to be authentic about who I am and to say what I want to say. I now feel good about me. It feels a good place to be.'

Halle Berry

The subtlety of self-sabotage

This behaviour is insidious and comes in many disguises. Our shadows encourage self-destructive behaviour that undermines our success. Many successful people say: 'When I get out of my own way, everything runs smoothly.'

One of the biggest factors in self-sabotage is not feeling deserving or worthy of success. However, we often need to be open to receive and to say 'bring it on'.

Do you lose a lot of weight, feel amazing, then slowly pile it back on? Do you start writing that novel and then quit? Do you have an amazing relationship, and walk away from it? Do you grow your nails, then bite them again?

If you have suffered trauma in your past, please do get professional help as this trauma keeps you stuck. If you have low self-esteem and a lack of confidence, you will find ways to ruin things. Many clients are unaware of how their actions or inaction affect their life; they begin to think they just don't have what it takes to achieve the success others have. You may sabotage your weight loss because deep down you are uncomfortable receiving attention or may feel vulnerable and more exposed. Perhaps having layers of fat keeps you feeling safe on some level. Maybe you say you want a raise or to change career, but apply for positions you know you are not qualified or suitable for, so, when you are rejected, you can tell others you tried but the job market is so hard right now. Perhaps you have children and the hours are incompatible, so you turn down the position offered rather than ask for the hours to be changed because deep down you are scared to go into something new.

Examine your motives

Perhaps you do want to start a business, but on some level you don't feel comfortable with success because your sister was made redundant last year and is struggling to find a job. You feel sensitive to her needs and subtly act in ways that will make you a failure, while convincing yourself that you are trying and taking action. If you have any fears or doubts or a lack of self-belief, your shadow will find a way to ensure that good things don't happen, or, if they do, that they don't last.

Perhaps you really want to meet someone and commit, but you are terrified of being hurt again, so on a subconscious level you attract those who are emotionally unavailable. The paradox is that if you lack self-confidence and have low self-esteem, you probably don't treat others badly – but I bet you treat yourself badly.

Design your own life

Remember: people will often try to manipulate you into their way of thinking, and acting in the way that serves them best. Confident people don't take part in these games; they approve of their own views and thoughts so they aren't affected by the manipulation of others. They detach themselves from it and do what works for them. Through sheer self-belief and enthusiasm they remove any doubts and remain responsible for their own development. Remember that it's OK to be successful, wealthy, healthy and content and to achieve whatever you want from life.

Sure, it is often tricky to ooze confidence when you don't feel it, but act as if you are confident and 'fake it till you make it'.

If you have spent years not being honest with yourself or with others, you must distinguish between what you can change and what you can't. By this I mean you cannot change the weather, or other people, or your age or height, so you can change within.

Negative self-scripts result in a lack of self-belief. Remember: low self-confidence has its origin in dysfunctional environments and harmful relationships that distort our thinking, feelings and behaviours. Therefore, be careful who you associate with as it's easy to develop unhealthy traits that will exacerbate your lack of confidence. Be careful about what you say to yourself as our subconscious hears and stores every word.

Do you truly want to dispel your irrational beliefs and the lies you tell yourself that you are not good enough? If so, slowly start discarding all the negative self-talk and replacing it with powerful, positive statements. Remember that all words are statements; if in the past you have mastered negative words, begin today to master positive words.

Here are some things to look out for when starting to design your own life.

Neurotic paradox

For the purposes of this book, this simply means that human behaviour is sometimes perpetuated indefinitely despite the fact that it is seriously self-defeating and self-punishing. It is the psychoanalytic term used to describe how some individuals cope with subconscious anxieties in a way that brings even more issues into their life. It's a way of avoiding anxiety, fear and pain that is itself maladaptive. We undermine our greatness by behaving in a way that makes us unhappy and then we blame external factors. We cling to our distorted perceptions that we are not good enough or lucky enough. In 12-step programmes, this is nicknamed 'stinking thinking'.

Delayed reactions

A drug addict uses a drug to feel numb, an alcoholic uses alcohol to get a warm, tingly sensation, and a food addict uses sugar to relieve their feelings – these are all hits. Once an untreated addict 'picks up' a substance (a drug, alcohol or sugar) or once they have 'acted out' in a process addiction (love or sex), they can't stop. If they are treated addicts (by this, I mean that they have been through a 12-step programme), they have alternatives, such as tools, resources and fellow addicts, to support them. If they prefer their drug of choice over a solution, they have made a conscious decision to do so. They may blame the 12-step programme for not working, but that is untrue: they consciously chose to go to the pub, or find a dealer, or go to a casino. The saying in 12-step programmes is: 'It works if you work it, so work it, you are worth it.'

Many blame the tools, their upbringing, friends, lack of confidence and myriad other excuses, but the bottom line is that many people punish themselves and go back into self-defeating behaviour – and they receive the pay-off they are looking for by using their drug of choice.

Your inner brain and body remember your habits and store the data. However, the pain is a delayed reaction. The hangover from binge drinking doesn't happen until the next day; the pain of overspending won't kick in until you max out your credit cards or lose your business; the pain from compulsive sex with strangers doesn't kick in until a scandal erupts, or the person you fall in love with walks away when you pass on a sexual infection. The pain of overeating sugar doesn't affect you until you have health issues as a result of your habit.

Never underestimate the consequences of repeating patterns that are self-defeating, self-punishing and toxic.

Euphoric recall

This is where you have a selective memory. You choose to remember the positive times and the highs. It is a little trick our primal mind plays on us where we screen out all negative incidents, feelings and thoughts, and remember only how good things feel (or felt).

- Your partner is constantly unfaithful, yet you stay with them as you remember how generous they are and how amazing your sex life is, and you choose to overlook their infidelity.
- You eat a lot of chocolate, and you feel heavier in your body. When you get a hit from the first bite of the next bar, you instantly choose to forget how upset you are that you can't fit into your favourite clothes.
- Your boss is demanding, offensive and bullies you. But you receive a big pay cheque so you overlook how abusive he is.

I asked **Holly Tucker**, co-founder of notonthehighstreet.com, about courage. Holly and business partner Sophie Cornish never gave up. Holly was diagnosed with a brain tumour at the age of 23, though she subsequently had the all-clear. They started the company from the kitchen table in 2006 while both bringing up small children, and by 2010 turnover hit £15 million. In 2012 they hired three very senior executives from Google, Amazon and PayPal.

Holly told me:

I have always been influenced by strong, prosperous women such as Dame Anita Roddick and Helena Morrissey. Now a ridiculously busy but proud business owner myself, I try to impart as much wisdom and advice to other women who are trying to achieve their own business dreams. When we hear some of the phenomenal success stories of our partners on notonthehighstreet.com, women who have been able to quit jobs that didn't satisfy them to turn their hobbies into fully-fledged businesses, or families who have been able to go on their first international holiday, it reinforces the belief I have had in notonthehighstreet.com since the beginning. We are not just helping the small businesses of the UK, we are changing the face of gifting. I feel so passionate about what we do, it was all the courage and motivation I needed to keep going. I admire many traits in people, especially enthusiasm, honesty and kindness. When we first tried to raise investment we were met with a lot of people who didn't understand us or share our vision; however, instead of giving up, we persisted until we met exactly the right investors who saw what we saw and helped take us to the next level. We had staff waiting to be paid and a business that was doing phenomenally well, and were outgrowing our financial provisions, which is why we needed the investment and we weren't ready to let it die. We kept going back to the city, doing endless presentations and praying for a miracle. Eventually it came; we met the perfect investors Spark, who shared our vision and supported us in those crucial early days. It was determination and vision that we believe led to our success. There is no destination when you are an entrepreneur, just the journey — so make sure you enjoy it all, warts and all!

Holly's top tips. *Do not let rejection knock you back — it happens to everyone and it's how you deal with it that matters. Sometimes rejection is a positive as it allows you to take the next step, which is a better one. Do not find excuses to give up; let motivation and passion keep you moving forward, whatever the obstacles.*

Annie's thoughts. *Holly's enthusiasm and motivation are contagious, not only in her own success but in helping others. Constant rejection made her more determined. Her assertiveness, courage and inner strength are a shining example to us all.*

When is the right time to implement change?

If you want something badly enough, you will make the time and prioritise your schedule to make it happen. If you don't want it badly enough, you will use any excuse not to do it.

Many years ago, I ran into an ex I hadn't had contact with for over 20 years. He asked: 'So, are you married?' I replied: 'I've been way too busy for that.'

He said: 'Annie, the Prime Minister is busy, but even he managed to squeeze in a marriage.' I burst out laughing, as I realised how futile it must have sounded and how right he was. It's amazing how we defend and hang on to our excuses. Losers blame everyone else and never take responsibility.

'I believe you make your day, make your life. So much of it is all about perception ... I have to accept my life and take responsibility for my choices.'

Brad Pitt

Be careful with your time, because one excuse I hear over and over is about the lack of it. Do you take responsibility for your time? Do you know where your time goes? Do you spend it wisely or is your time in debt? It isn't about *finding* time for important things; it's about *making* time. Being busy and being productive are two different things. Ask for help if you need it; don't be a martyr. Value your time the same way you value money. It is a precious commodity.

Once it's gone, it's gone. People will rarely value your time unless you value it. When you forget things, are late for appointments, are unprepared, take on too much or are not smart with your time, others will take advantage and you can then feel frustrated, which will chip away at your confidence. Failing to plan is planning to fail. Create a daily time journal – it is very revealing and the facts don't lie.

Five things you can do straight away

Have you worked out the answer yet? When is the right time to implement change? It's right now! Here are five things you can do right away.

1. Make a list (this is a highly effective exercise I use with all my corporate clients)

Firstly write down all the tasks, big and small, in your mental inbox. Don't analyse these too much to begin with, just get them down on paper. Then, when the list is more or less complete, split the tasks into three categories:

1. What is urgent and important?

2. What is urgent but not important?

3. What is important but not urgent?

Important tasks have deadlines in the future, but they must be done. Don't let them pile up, as they will end up urgent *and* important.

Urgent tasks are deadline-based. These are often driven by other people, and their urgency is not always related to their importance.

Categorising and prioritising your 'to do' list like this will make it seem a lot less daunting.

2. Be ruthless about scheduling your priorities

Make sure you differentiate between important and urgent. Do what you dislike first – don't spend time worrying about it; just do it.

3. Set aside uninterrupted time

At home or at work, focus on the tasks in hand and break down any monster tasks into chunks. Value your time and set boundaries with others.

4. Organise your home and work space so you don't waste any time searching for things

You must make sure you are not putting off what needs to be done to achieve your visions, dreams and goals. Think about how you are undervaluing your time by giving it away. Stay focused on your goals and make smarter choices about your time. Ask yourself why you make excuses rather than changes. Remember that when you abuse your time, you are stealing from yourself, stealing from your future. I recommend you read Duncan Bannatyne's excellent book *How To Be Smart With Your Time* .

5. Recognise your habits for what they are

Take control of your life and emotions. Start focusing on clarity of thought and new attitudes, so you have confidence in your ability and become selective in the memories you choose to value. When you don't value yourself, your perception is distorted because you are motivated by fear. You have an inability to trust your intuition because not only is it clouded by anxiety, but you also feel the need to follow blindly what others tell you, becoming overly submissive, which often leads to feeling even less positively about yourself.

Take a pad, and:

   a. list on the left-hand side of a page all your negative habits
   b. list on the right-hand side how they manifest in your life today
   c. list on the left-hand side of another page all your positive habits
   d. list on the right-hand side how they manifest in your life today.

This will help you to become aware of the habits that create negative consequences, and to master the new habits to create positive consequences.

The implementing change checklist

Next, take a look at this checklist and make some longer-term changes.

   ☐ Take care of your appearance and health.
   ☐ Value your time and energy.
   ☐ Be passionate about your goals.
   ☐ Be tenacious.
   ☐ Don't keep comparing and despairing.
   ☐ Value your strengths.
   ☐ Stand up for yourself.
   ☐ Approve of yourself.
   ☐ Walk through your fears.
   ☐ Polish your social skills.

- ☐ Have a generous spirit.
- ☐ Actively seek opportunities.
- ☐ Think outside of the box.
- ☐ Seek challenges.
- ☐ Learn to listen and listen to learn.
- ☐ Opt for being effective rather than being right.
- ☐ Only spend time with positive people.
- ☐ Detach from difficult and negative personalities.
- ☐ Embrace change.
- ☐ Put principles before personalities.
- ☐ Stay focused on your goals.
- ☐ Be open and flexible.
- ☐ Have a heightened self-awareness.
- ☐ Focus on self-improvement.
- ☐ Trust your talents.
- ☐ Respect others' values and principles.

A thought is a thought, and a thought can be changed.

People with low self-esteem and a lack of confidence are often motivated by feelings of inadequacy that stop them from going for it. Distorted and irrational thinking leads you to believe you can't trust anyone because everyone wants to take advantage of you, which is not always the case.

'The greatest discovery of all time is that a person can change their future by merely changing their attitude.'

Oprah Winfrey

When you have low self-confidence you generally have more ambivalence than people with high self-confidence. So are you ready to tell yourself something different? If you define yourself by what's happened in the past, you will keep on repeating the past. Are you ready to make new choices? You can unlearn your fear by choosing to be positive and realising that the only thing that can harm you is fear itself. Are you ready to commit today to start banishing fear or negativity in its entirety and all unwanted, inappropriate thoughts and symptoms, replacing them with good feelings and positive thoughts?

SUMMARY. HAVING THE COURAGE TO BE YOUR OWN HERO

◆ Focus on one change for 28 days – keep repeating the new positive statement until it feels natural before moving on to the next. Some need more than 28 days to kick in as some false realities you have woven may take longer to unravel.

◆ You must spend time with positive people who champion you. Remember: you emulate those you associate with.

◆ Passion and motivation are intrinsic driving forces that can stop you being stuck. Be clear about your purpose for making changes. It's too easy to lose motivation.

◆ Spend a short amount of time every day listening to something inspirational or speak to an inspirational friend.

◆ Set boundaries.

◆ Keep your light of awareness on, so you can make smarter choices in life.

◆ Fire your internal committee, and watch out for the lingering saboteur.

◆ Drop the excuses – none of them are good enough.

◆ Be smart with your time.

◆ Stop analysing and take action instead – you will find your courage grows. If you want courage to have an important conversation, plan and practise what you want to say. If you wait until everything is perfect, you will never make any changes or have the courage to do anything. Successful people are not crazily impulsive, but once they have decided to take action and make changes, they *do it*.

A call to action

1. The lessons I have learned about courage are:

....

....

2. A person or situation I have needed courage around is:

....

....

3. I have been fearful because:

....

....

4. The excuses I might make to avoid facing a person or situation are:

....

....

5. The steps I will take to overcome my fears and build my courage muscles are:

....

....

ANNIE'S CONFIDENCE-BOOSTERS

◆ Start small, start somewhere, start now.
◆ Develop faith in yourself.
◆ Consider what is the worst that can happen.
◆ Visualise the outcome you desire.
◆ Say over and over 'I can, I will'.

Part 2. The seven secrets of self-confident people

Secret no. 1

SELF-RESPECT

Successful people consider themselves important

'As much as anybody else in the entire universe, you deserve your love and affection.'

Buddha

Why do I lack self-respect?

What is fed into your subconscious between the ages of nought to five is done so without your consent or knowledge. As you internalise everything as true, you record this as your own assessment of yourself. If you were fed negativity, it may well have created havoc in every area of your life. Many people who haven't been taught to love and accept themselves at an early age keep themselves small and steeped in fear in order to avoid rejection and disappointments. That's surviving, not living. Few are taught to love and accept every part of themselves and value and honour their own views and instincts. From an early age you listen to your inner critic, which feeds you lies and often tells you that you are not good enough.

Unfortunately, many of us grew up with parents, teachers and 'frenemies' (enemies disguised as friends) who flagged up our shortcomings rather than our assets. Many of us had parents and teachers who were critical of themselves and therefore projected that on to us by criticising us.

Even if you were not the most gifted or talented child growing up and didn't do well at school, if you had parents and teachers championing, motivating, supporting and encouraging you, your self-respect would have been high and you would have chosen to believe that anything was possible, and that through studying, working hard and staying focused and disciplined you could be successful.

'We ought to celebrate our individuality and not be ashamed of it.'

Johnny Depp

Most of us are brought up to avoid conflict and do as we are told, so when we grow up we stay small and play safe; this crushes our self-respect and often we build up resentment over time. Many people have been programmed as children by the demands of society, family, religion and education. These can cause us either to be too nice or to be a rebel – both of which are damaging to our self-respect.

To obtain self-respect, feel that you are important, and raise your confidence you must look inside and ponder your shortcomings, rather than deny them. When you find the courage to own your truth, everything will improve in your life.

The art of self-worth

When you have self-respect, you are secure in yourself because you have cultivated the self-confidence to tackle whatever life throws at you. Also, you never feel that someone else's success diminishes your self-worth. A lack of self-confidence, self-esteem and self-respect doesn't make you bad. We have all been there and have made mistakes. Changes are not always easy, but it is essential that you reframe the way you think about yourself and start becoming aware that you are important.

When you feel important, you become authentic and respect your own values, instead of compromising them to gain external validation and violating your sense of right and wrong. This behaviour chips away at your self-confidence.

Undervaluing your qualities is one of the worst punishments you can inflict on yourself. The bottom line is that, by respecting yourself, you extend yourself and honour your own wishes.

You shoot yourself in the foot by placing a low value on yourself, as it immediately demonstrates that you don't trust your abilities or believe in yourself. If you don't believe in yourself, how can you expect others to believe in you?

Advertise your strengths

When you gain self-respect, you lose the ridiculous belief that you are unlovable, inadequate, unworthy or incompetent. Possessing self-respect means not allowing others to manipulate you and not being swayed or seduced by others who only have their own interests at heart.

Stop believing that others see the negative aspects that you believe you have. Stop being so prickly over little things that are not even necessarily directed at you. Leave behind the negativity that often leads to frustration, anxiety, anger, resentment and disappointment. Advertise your assets, rather than displaying your weaknesses.

Emine Ali Rushton answers some questions on self-respect and why we need to know we are important. She has worked across a plethora of publications, including *Vogue*, *GQ* and *Elle*, and is now beauty and well-being editor of *Psychologies Magazine*.

Emine told me:

My parents are an inspiration as they came to the UK with nothing and built several successful businesses. My mother had three children before she had turned 25, and is firm, fair and very funny. I want my reputation to be strong because I am naturally ambitious. My family motivate me — as the breadwinner, I want to be a great role model for my daughter, and I'm more comfortable in the workplace while my husband is a natural homemaker. It was a challenge realising my dream job had become vacant literally weeks after having my first child. I struggled for days, wanting to apply, but part of me was thinking it was insane! I met the editor, talked candidly about the role, and my experience, and we worked out a solution that was mutually beneficial. It is crucial to have self-respect and consider yourself important enough never to allow anyone to tell you anything is impossible. Sometimes things are just not right, and that is different; but never rest on your laurels. If you really want something, give it your best shot. The older I get the more increasingly fatalistic I become — I believe we are let down for good reasons and it's not necessarily apparent why until much later on. Many times I thought I'd hit rock bottom career-wise, only to realise bigger and better opportunities were waiting around the corner. In my industry you are only as good as your ideas — networking can get you so far, but to progress further and build a strong reputation, you must continually innovate and produce content which makes people sit up and take notice, content which you are ultimately proud to put your name to.

Emine's top tips. *When it's done, it's done — but if you did it wrong, always be the first to apologise. Graciousness is hugely undervalued. Be generous, kind and have self-respect, as those traits will take you far.*

Annie's thoughts. *Remember: when you have self-respect you will be your own best supporter and be clear about the outcomes you want to create. Focus your energy on achieving your goals regardless of the obstacles placed in your path and the rejections along the way.*

Are you disguising low self-respect?

If your teachers or parents insisted on rules you had to obey, and maybe these rules included putting the other person's needs first, it is likely that you have learnt to respect everyone else but disrespect yourself.

Meet Mike.

Mike was a good-looking 32-year-old. He had dated Steve for six months and felt something wasn't right. All was great for the first 12 weeks, then Mike started modifying his actions and watching what he was saying as Steve constantly criticised him. He felt he had to walk on eggshells to avoid a confrontation, especially after Steve had a few drinks, and he acted submissively without knowing he was. Steve would say: 'Why are you so quiet, what's going on?' Mike would say: 'Nothing, everything's fine.'

Mike felt pressured into going places and seeing friends he didn't want to. He never wanted to rock the boat with Steve because he feared Steve would get angry. His whole thinking became dominated by fear, criticism, humiliation and rejection. Mike found himself ignoring his intuition and pleasing Steve. Friends were asking him why he was afraid to speak up. He sacrificed his psychological well-being in order to keep Steve happy.

After some hypnotherapy sessions and working with me on strengthening his inner confidence muscles, he was able to stand up to Steve and own his power. He left Steve the following month.

Mike's top tips. *Don't give your power away by bending yourself to others.*

Be clear from day one about what your needs are, and take the risk of losing someone if they are not happy with you being confident.

Annie's thoughts. *Many people allow themselves to be controlled by others because they do not recognise the treatment they are receiving as 'emotional bullying'. We allow this abuse to continue if we are punishing ourselves; if we felt good about ourselves and had self-respect, we would not allow this to continue.*

Each one of us has the ability and right to be who we want and to do what we want. If we tap into our generator, our energy within, we will find it is either potential or kinetic. Potential energy is passive energy, waiting to be used; kinetic energy is active energy, which *is* being used. Most of our choices are made unconsciously, so raise your consciousness: instead of using 'should' or 'must', I suggest you turn it into 'I choose'. When I hear 'should' from my clients, I detect a subtle reluctance on their part to take responsibility for themselves.

> 'Stop letting people who do so little for you control your mind, feelings and emotions.'
>
> Will Smith

Tap into your inner strength

I spoke to **Lynne Franks** – PR guru and the inspiration for the huge TV hit *Absolutely Fabulous* – about self-respect. Lynne advises on market positioning strategies for corporations, including Cisco, Google, HSBC, Starbucks, McDonald's and Danone, and is also a TV personality and bestselling author.

Lynne told me:

It is essential to have self-respect so you don't let other people's opinions get the better of you. I know who I am and I don't worry what others think. Ego is a dangerous animal, both good and bad, and especially so in the public arena, but the important thing is not to take what others say too seriously. I attribute my success to my intuition, determination, loving people, creativity, empathy, passion and being good at what I do. I always knew I wanted to work for myself, be creatively fulfilled, write and contribute to society — the rest was in the hands of a greater energy than me, but I knew what I was good at and what I enjoyed.

Lynn's top tips. *Have self-respect so you do not seek approval and validation from others. Follow your intuition and have the willingness to listen and be gracious enough to contribute to society.*

Annie's thoughts. *Lynne doesn't worry what others think of her as she has self-respect and honours herself and her own opinions.*

You do not need outside approval and you do not need to take anyone else's inventory. You need to be who you are, and to know that who you are is more than enough. You cannot allow your internal committee to linger and distort your image of yourself. You must no longer neglect your needs and wants, otherwise continual devaluation will cause you constant challenges in all areas of your life. When we lack confidence, it is often due to limiting beliefs from childhood. Ask yourself – is this thought helpful? Change the thoughts you think and the words you speak, and stop feeling obliged to go along with what someone else thinks. Quietly affirm to yourself that you will define your own reality.

You have a choice, so it's essential to break your emotional dependence on friends, family, colleagues and bosses and instead build emotional space between yourself and them.

Every time you put someone else's needs and wants before your own, you are reaffirming to yourself that you are not worthy. You are in effect saying to the other person, 'You are more important than me. I am not as important as you.'

'Poor is the man whose pleasure depends upon the permission of another.'

Madonna

Give yourself a break – I don't mean you should rest on your laurels, but don't whip yourself either! Remember that you are doing the very best you can with the knowledge you have today. There are no rights or wrongs: 'it is as it is' and 'you get it when you get it'.

With a strong sense of belief, confidence, strong communication skills and assertiveness techniques, you can gain self-respect and bring about tangible changes.

Be in awe of yourself; it's crucial that you believe you are important at all times. You must learn to take your eyes off everyone else and focus on yourself. You are responsible for your own joy and happiness, your own discomfort and your own upset.

'I like me, I think I am kinda cool.'

Whoopi Goldberg

Self-respect and self-care are your responsibility to yourself. No-one can do it for you. You must stop the blaming, the oppression and the constant victimisation, and own your power. You must stay focused 24/7 on your positive traits and not your negative ones.

Fine-tune your behaviour

When your behaviour is challenged or questioned, do you hide behind your ego, by:

- denying?
- blaming?
- projecting your thoughts and feelings on to others?
- rationalising?
- justifying?
- defending?

Dig inside to find these hidden treasures:

- simplicity
- patience
- compassion.

A few of my clients start off with a slight resistance to making changes. It is a common defence mechanism that holds us back from new experiences and success. If we resist change, it can have painful, even lethal, consequences (if, for example, you fail to address an addiction or eating disorder).

Let's meet **James**, who turned perfectionism into excellence. James is 34 and works for a Swiss bank in the City. He had strong feelings of anxiety about presentations, but somehow he managed to bumble his way through. He said he would go nights without sleeping before the pitch. James's father used to shout at him when he made mistakes and he was ashamed if he wasn't perfect, so he didn't stretch himself or maximise his potential.

James constantly feared that when he pitched he would be criticised. I explained to him that his colleagues and clients were there to be informed, educated and inspired, not to criticise him. What evidence did he have that they would? He was stuck in his past and allowing his inner child to run his life. His belief system was distorted.

Release shame

Being pulled up for making mistakes is what formed James's perfectionism. After a few sessions of hypnotherapy and coaching, he started to see risk as exciting, and finally had the willingness to go beyond his comfort zone.

He no longer allowed the criticism and negativity he had endured as a child to knock him off balance. He no longer wanted old beliefs to run his life. He entered the palace of opportunities during hypnotherapy, as I offered him many positive statements, encouraging and supporting him to let go of:

- self-doubt, self-disapproval and self-loathing
- his need for validation
- fear-based thoughts.

I replaced these beliefs with:

- 'I approve of myself'
- 'I am more than enough'
- 'I walk through my fears'.

James said:

When I first came to see Annie, I honestly thought we would have one session and that would be it. I had no idea we would have any reason to dig deeper. Annie gave me insights into things I had never thought about and, with a heightened awareness, I feel more confident, and OK with making mistakes. The paradox is now that I am not bothered about seeking approval, I get more than I ever got before. I also find work colleagues are way more respectful to me and well, yes, much has changed. And as I have changed so has my relationship, as my girlfriend seems to like this new-found respect. Thanks Annie.

James's top tips. *Build self-respect so you become self-reliant and stop judging yourself. Our parents did the best they could, but you can't keep buying into all their opinions or blaming them for what happened when you were a child.*

Annie's thoughts. *These habits were established early. However, because James created his experiences, and these experiences were his context, only he could choose to make changes. He had to build his self-respect and not allow fear to continue to run his life.*

There is an expiry date on blaming your parents for steering you in the wrong direction. The moment you are old enough you need to take the wheel, as the responsibility lies within you.'

J. K. Rowling

Can't or won't?

'You cannot make decisions based on fear and the possibility of what might happen.'

Michelle Obama

Risk is a necessary element in our self-development. If we want to grow spiritually, emotionally and mentally, and raise our confidence, we must be willing to take risks. Why do we constantly think 'I can't' and fear taking risks so much?

- We fear we may achieve our dream and then decide it's not what we want.
- We fear failure as we feel it will be way too painful.
- We worry we may lose what we have.

Why are you defensive about your fear and old, limiting beliefs? Why do you expend time and energy holding on to what doesn't work for you? Why explain to yourself and convince others that things won't work? In order to transcend fear you have to walk through it. Why are you believing your own propaganda? Many say to me 'I can't', meaning that they don't want to take responsibility for their decisions or their actions. They are refusing to and unwilling to do so. I suggest they change the words to 'I won't' or 'I am unwilling' as this changes the whole experience and is far more honest.

It's important you are completely honest with yourself, that you learn how to be comfortable with who you are and not be scared of tapping into your inner strength and self-worth. By becoming resilient, having faith and trusting, we find the willingness within ourselves to make changes and treat ourselves with respect and dignity.

It's essential for any parents reading this to know that it's your duty to encourage your children to try new things and not be afraid of making mistakes. I hear so many clients tell me they were shamed or scolded for making mistakes. Children must be taught that errors are unavoidable and it's perfectly acceptable to get things wrong, especially when learning. Shaming them will severely erode their confidence and affect their relationships both at work and personally.

When children are learning to walk and fall down, time and time again we are patient and hug them and encourage them. So why is it any different when they are older? James was resisting success on a subconscious level and, unfortunately, whatever we resist persists because we give so much energy to it. You must own your power, your innate worth, so remember to keep saying 'I can' and 'I will'.

Cultivate a relationship with yourself

In order to raise your self-esteem and self-confidence and to feel important, you need to take time and get to know yourself. You need to have self-discipline and trust your intuition so you become your own best friend. Why? Because you are important.

Basic meditation

The first thing I suggest is to spend five minutes daily meditating. Keep it simple. Set your alarm for five minutes and unplug all phones. Sit upright in a chair and close your eyes and slowly count from one to ten, over and over until the time is up. The purpose of the counting is to override your busy mind to stay focused. When you start, don't worry if you have a chattering mind. The key is to do this daily as a discipline. It will make a huge difference to your day.

This will take you into your internal world, and help you develop and strengthen a relationship with yourself, to connect you with your feelings. Have the courage to look within and explore what is going on, to remove yourself from the busyness of life and connect to yourself. Let your breathing slow down. Soothe your nervous system. Let your soul sing.

Remember: your worries are cognitive distortions and not easy to give up, so make this a regular practice – no excuses! Let this daily practice become as automatic as brushing your teeth.

SUMMARY. WAKING YOUR SELF-RESPECT

◆ Flush out any negative thoughts you have about yourself. Self-respect is an attitude. Be reliable with yourself – do what you promise yourself you will do. Set and achieve goals as this will help your confidence and self-respect skyrocket and you can achieve what you put your mind to.

◆ Remind yourself you are loving and lovable even if you make mistakes. Honour and value your principles, listen to and respect your inner voice. Fire your internal committee.

◆ Do not allow anyone to dictate what you do or manipulate you into doing what is good for them. Respect your own needs and wants, and do and say what feels right to you. You will start believing that you are not less than anyone else; you will feel at one with yourself and equal to everyone else. Advertise your strengths, not your weaknesses.

◆ Choose to be kind, tolerant and compassionate with yourself, give up your excuses, and stop living your life according to other people's expectations. Meditate for five minutes a day.

A call to action

1. The lessons I have learned about self-respect are:

....

....

2. A person or situation I have needed self-respect around is:

....

....

3. I have felt disrespected because:

....

....

4. The excuses I might make to avoid facing this disrespect are:

....

....

5. The steps I will take to build self-respect are:

....

....

ANNIE'S CONFIDENCE-BOOSTERS FOR SELF-RESPECT

◆ Support yourself with positive self-talk when things feel challenging.
◆ Process your emotions.
◆ Express your needs – do not repress them.
◆ Keep a success journal.
◆ Pay attention to how you respond to others.

Secret no. 2

SELF-APPROVAL

Self-confident people are kind to their mind and banish their inner critics

'To be yourself in a world that is constantly trying to make you something else is the greatest accomplishment.'
Ralph Waldo Emerson

The blueprint for self-approval

People tend to get confused between self-approval and ego. It's always essential to keep in mind that truly confident people do not need to judge, criticise or bully others. Successful people do not need to justify their existence nor be subject to interrogation. They disapprove of pretension and hypocrisy. Self-approval, intention and self-belief are powerful factors.

Successful people appreciate themselves – including all their faults and foibles. They approve and appreciate their self-worth, take pride in their accomplishments and do not set themselves unrealistic expectations. When others do not choose them for a job or as a partner, they do not take it personally because they know others' likes or dislikes, approval or rejection are not tied up with their own values and emotions.

'I began thinking, "Do I want to please others or please Mary first?" I started pleasing Mary. I can't please everyone. Be the best you can be. I was drawing *negative people to me with my negative thoughts. You have got to change the way you think about yourself.'*

Mary J. Blige

The comments and actions of others are merely information about that person's views and opinions.

The paradox is that the more you look to be liked, the less authentic you become and then the less you are liked. Seeking approval is not a good look, and when you do this you are giving away your ability to feel your own feelings, make your own decisions, and think your own thoughts. Successful people have fears and have inner critics, but they don't allow these to destabilise them.

Inspiration and purpose

Successful people are visionaries, and you can be too if you want to be. Even if you are not interested in being an entrepreneur, you can be much more successful in your personal and professional relationships by mastering self-approval. As the gorgeous Jessie J sings: 'It's not about the money.'

You can become rich in inner belief, confidence, strength, kindness, wisdom and knowledge once you build a strong relationship with yourself.

Self-approval refers to a temporary approbation of the self at a particular period of time. In self-approval, the focus is primarily on the value of one's behaviour rather than the value of one's self (this is self-acceptance). You can have a sense of self-acceptance and yet still not have self-approval.

Ask yourself the questions listed below.

- Why would you need to ask permission from someone else to be who you are?
- Why would you believe others know what's best for you?
- Why would you believe everyone has your best interests at heart?

- Why would you ask advice from others who don't have what you want?
- Why would you look for approval outside of yourself?
- Why would you compare and despair?
- Why would you pretend to be anyone else, except yourself?
- Why would you give your power away to others?
- Why would you not believe what you believe?
- Why would you go cap in hand to somebody and place their opinion above your own?

Banishing your inner critic

I asked **Carla Buzasi** about self-approval. Carla is editor-in-chief of the UK edition of *The Huffington Post*, a major news website, and responsible for strategy, brand-building and content across AOL's network, as well as for the relationship with the *Post* in the US. Carla has won numerous awards and is a regular contributor to programmes on ITV, Sky and the BBC.

Carla told me:

Those closest to me describe me as driven, emotional and sensitive. My parents told me to do something I loved, and have always been on hand to give advice and to champion me. Trying to be the very best I possibly can motivates me, a trait honed over years of family card games. I really admire those with passion and who lead from the front with confidence. If my inner critic shows itself, I overcome it by surrounding myself with positive people who help me put things in perspective. When I was younger I had no master plan, but I did always know I wanted to write for a living. I now oversee a team of 25 editors, and a pool of over 3,000 contributing bloggers, which is wonderful. I have made hundreds of mistakes along the way, but I do possess self-approval, and learn from both the good and the bad. There is a small part of me that believes most things happen for a reason.

Carla's top tips. *Work like you don't need the money, love like you've never been hurt, dance like no-one's watching, sing like no-one's listening, and live like there is no tomorrow and approve of yourself.*

Annie's thoughts. *Carla clearly approves of herself. Like everyone, she occasionally has a weak moment, but she doesn't fall into thinking 'poor me' or 'I'm not good enough' – she surrounds herself with positive people and gets everything back into perspective.*

'We are not on this earth to accumulate victories, things and experiences, but to be whittled and sandpapered until what is left is who we truly are.'

Arianna Huffington

Our primary purpose in life is to work on our relationship with ourselves and then we can inspire others to do the same, as we can't give away what we don't have.

Are you investing in yourself?

Many of us don't feel worthy of investing time and energy in ourselves. Many of us punish and abuse ourselves with self-sabotaging behaviours, putting ourselves down, neglecting ourselves, criticising ourselves and allowing others to criticise us. Many of us self-medicate by drinking, smoking, overeating and metaphorically whipping ourselves for not being perfect. Many say: 'I should have done this and I should have done that.' That word 'should' is toxic, negative, shaming and cruel, so don't use it on yourself and don't allow anyone else to use it on you either.

If you postpone self-approval until you truly accept yourself and meet your goals, you will waste time and energy, because even when you achieve all your goals they could be taken from you at any time.

Nothing is guaranteed in life so we need to approve of ourselves whether or not we have fulfilled our ambitions.

Our self-confidence is shaped by internal and external factors. Firstly, you have limiting beliefs and behaviours that you have practised for many years. Secondly, you may have had parents, teachers, partners and institutions enforcing these beliefs and behaviours verbally and non-verbally every day. In addition, many people broadcast additional negative messages that you may buy into. Stop trying so hard to be what others want and expect you to be. When you are insecure, your ego kicks in and you seek constant approval.

Approval addiction

Approval addiction is an epidemic of the 21st century. Anything that controls us and becomes a 'fix' is an addiction. Therefore, if you need reassurance on any level that you are good enough or acceptable in someone else's eyes, you are without doubt an approval addict, a junkie dependent on others' opinions, thoughts and blessings.

'If you don't approve of yourself — if you don't realise your self-worth and your own value — then somebody else will see that and take advantage of it.'

Arianna Huffington

Working in film and TV for many years, I have witnessed first-hand many famous people who received adulation, recognition and admiration from millions globally. However, it was apparent that despite this many of these people had no peace, serenity or self-approval because they self-destructed through addiction. This caused constant emotional turmoil and mental turbulence.

Identify your patterns

Many people seek much more than loud applause, fake kisses and media attention.

They have a deep need for self-approval, but instead of searching within, they look outside for validation and constant assurance.

They yearn and need to be loved by everybody at any cost. This is a quick fix, and quick fixes wear off just as quickly. There is less need for society to approve of you when you approve of yourself. Sure, it's always nice to be appreciated and respected, but you don't need to be a slave to social approval. Approval feeds your deepest and strongest desires, and when you internalise negative feedback you often start to doubt your inner worth, which will threaten your sense of security.

As an actress and model, I loved the constant applause, attention and accolades, especially from men. It fed my ego very nicely, but it didn't satisfy my deep hunger for self-approval. No amount of press cuttings, pay cheques or adulation could ever compete with the self-confidence and self-approval I possess today.

Annie's quiz

Please tick the statements that apply to you. Be rigorously honest with yourself.

- ☐ I disapprove of and judge my inadequacies harshly.
- ☐ I justify and defend myself to create a better opinion of myself.
- ☐ I hold back from stating my opinion until I know what others think.
- ☐ I worry about how I look and how I come across.
- ☐ I feel a knot in my stomach when confronting someone.
- ☐ I am always thinking of a witty response when speaking to others.
- ☐ I need my parents/partner/tutor/boss to be proud of me.
- ☐ I obsess on what I am doing wrong, rather than what I am doing right.
- ☐ I am pretty tough on myself if I don't achieve my goals.
- ☐ I am impatient and intolerant of myself if I get things wrong.

☐ I am intolerant of my weaknesses.
☐ I am impatient with myself when learning new skills.
☐ I am unsure if I have made the right choice.
☐ I need others to validate my choices.

Scores

0–3 ticks

Not bad at all. You pretty much approve of yourself, and if you are being fiercely honest here, then you just need to look at why you have these odd moments of weakness and don't trust yourself. Devise a strategy like Carla Buzasi's to reframe things.

4–8 ticks

Let's cut to the chase: it's clear you have a low sense of self-approval and what others think is of vital importance to you, regardless of who they are. I want you to dig deep and appraise yourself on the other questions. Look at whether they also apply to you. I imagine you project an image of assurance that manages to fool some of the people, some of the time, yet inside you feel inadequate. I imagine your image is very important, and you have a deep-rooted need to be loved.

More than eight ticks

Well, this demonstrates that you are someone who appears to believe you have no right to occupy space in the world. You recycle the opinions of others. You give away your power and, through a fear of being abandoned, you abandon yourself. You are too critical and harsh on yourself. The bottom line is that you view yourself as unworthy and unacceptable and you reject yourself by seeking others' approval. How would it be to be loved for being you, rather than for having an amazing body, a fabulous title, a great home, artistic skills or a sports medal? How amazing would it be to approve of yourself so much that you attract people who love and respect you for being you?

Mind your own business

If you take a moment to step back and figure out what you need to give yourself, you could stop searching for it from others. Why don't you make it a mission as from today to quit focusing on other people's opinions of you and instead invest attention in what you think of yourself? Sometimes others tell us what we want to hear, which is not always the truth.

- Who gives others the right to decide what's right for you?
- Who made others the 'master of your destiny'?
- Who gave others permission to decide who you are?
- Who told others they knew better than you?
- Who told others that their opinions were facts?

You are a consenting adult, so why are you checking with others about what rules you ought to play by?

If you present a mask to the world, not only is that dishonest but it will also erode your confidence. It's not the real you that you are representing; it's a stranger. How futile to walk around with a false identity to gain approval. I know from my own experience that it is utterly exhausting, so please mind your own business, be yourself and get real.

You need to grasp that finding self-approval means finding what is rightly yours and making it your business to invest in it and own it. It's no-one else's business how you feel, act, behave or think. As long as you are not hurting anyone by being who you are, then what on earth is the problem?

Kick the self-criticism habit

Most of us – perhaps as many as nine out of ten – criticise and judge ourselves. These unkind and cruel behaviours you continue to repeat day after day stem from childhood. But you wouldn't get away with speaking to friends the way you speak to yourself. Lacking self-confidence and self-esteem, you will make incorrect judgements and evaluations of yourself. It means you belittle, berate and slam yourself for not being good enough. The paradox is that you affirm that you are not good enough and that there is something inherently wrong with you, and you then start to convince yourself you are a loser. This constant self-loathing and self-battering can lead to you feeling depressed or stuck or hopeless. It is estimated that we make between 300 and 400 self-evaluations a day, and most of those, maybe as many as 80%, are negative.

One theory is that self-criticism is anger turned inwards. Many are too insecure to let out their anger so they end up becoming hostile but internalising it. That's dangerous as it can lead to depression and anxiety. Another theory is that those who self-criticise are doing so from guilt and subconsciously shielding themselves against criticism from others, as if thinking 'You can't say anything I don't already say to myself.'

Discover how anger develops

Hatred, contempt, rigidity, malice, jealousy, distrust, sarcasm, cynicism, suspicion, envy, anxiety, contempt, intolerance, self-pity, resentment, discontent, fear, frustration, self-righteousness, self-defiance, criticism and sulking are all manifestations of anger. Sometimes anger is the result of fear, and some people are not always aware of what makes them fearful. If you feel any of the above on a regular basis, pause and ask yourself: 'What is it about my self-worth that makes me feel so angry?'

'Use failure as a stepping stone. Close the door on your past. Don't dwell on your mistakes, or let them have any of your time, energy or space.'

Johnny Cash

Harness your worn-out behaviours

Why stress yourself by telling yourself you are not good enough? Stop giving away your power by looking for outside approval. Have a think about how you can change the circumstances in which you find yourself, and then consider how you can handle the situation if it happens again.

Learn – find a new strategy, have a moan for five minutes, then move on. Sure, we all mess up and make mistakes, big deal. That's life. Successful people ensure they don't repeat mistakes: they learn, move forward and refuse to dwell on it. Instead of sitting in the self-loathing box, jump into the high self-esteem and high self-confidence box and get yourself a positive outlook and a new set of beliefs. Stop searching for your weak points and instead look for your strengths and assets. Once you turn your inner critic into your best friend, you don't take what others say so personally. Learn to shrug off other people's opinions unless they are helpful.

Take a good look and see whether you can identify anyone who is perfect, with no flaws. Tell me this: if you don't notice the flaws in those you are comparing yourself with, why do you imagine they notice yours?

Unlock your potential

Ask yourself what a loser looks like and how a loser behaves, and then ask yourself if that is you. Keep challenging your inner critic with reality. If you don't get the job you want, and you criticise yourself, look back at the jobs you *did* get rather than beating yourself up.

Think outside the box. If the job or the house or the partner you wanted didn't come your way as you planned, perhaps the universe has something much better coming your way.

Write down in your journal all that you are grateful for and all your achievements, and read it each time you berate yourself.

Make your goal each day to improve a habit, a thought, a behaviour, rather than criticising yourself. Challenge and change your inner critic by making positive affirmations every day for four weeks and then keep it going consistently so you create new neural pathways in your brain. I promise you that your anxiety levels will decrease and your confidence and self-esteem will rocket. I can't emphasise enough how imperative it is to keep on top of this.

> 'I've realised that it's time for me to show my audience that you don't have to be perfect to achieve your dreams.'
>
> Katy Perry

Christopher Maloney appeared on *The X Factor* auditions in 2012 and told everyone that he had previously torn up his application form five years running. He listened to everyone telling him not to apply because he would embarrass himself. Of course, they all knew best! He didn't possess self-approval so he believed them. Then his grandmother persuaded him to try. He started singing, and the audience gave him two standing ovations. Remember: before you allow anyone to judge you, consider whether they are flawless.

Say to yourself over and over again 'I can' and 'I will'. Your subconscious asks your conscious mind to focus on the things that will help support your inner critic. The more you lack approval, the more you believe it, and the more your mind actively sets out to prove it. Beware!

Stretch your mind

I asked **Michael Van Clarke**, one of the world's leading hairdressers, about self-approval. Michael has won 17 awards and at the age of 19 he had his first *Vogue* spread. His clients include political leaders, rock stars, Hollywood A-listers and nine royal families. Michael is described by the press as a technically brilliant creative genius.

Michael told me:

> I am inspired by anyone doing something really well or innovatively. I came from a relatively poor background and at an

early age was inspired by biographies of successful people. If I asked my Greek mother for something beyond the family budget she'd always say, 'Who do you think we are, Onassis?' So I read up on him and more recently on tycoons such as Steve Jobs. Leonardo da Vinci has long inspired me for his sheer excellence and originality across so many disciplines of art and science. I am always motivated by a desire to realise more of myself and to make a worthwhile contribution, to create something better. Usually if you stick with it the landscape changes. It's always so attractive when people have integrity, a sense of humour and are generous in spirit — I really admire those traits. Rejection used to bother me more in the early days, but from a business sales point of view now, I fully believe in myself and do not seek approval, so a rejection just tells me my communication isn't good enough. The most difficult challenge I have experienced was probably a mid-life crisis that involved a lot of personal and business loss, and emotional and physical injury. It was a deep dark time, but coming out of it I saw it as a turning point in my own development and awareness. I have a lot of courage, determination, integrity and resilience and I can honestly say those have been the main attributes for my success.

Michael's top tips. *Never, never, never give up. Do not be too impatient or afraid to sit through the painful stages of progress and development. Don't give up too easily. Approve of yourself and keep going, no matter what.*

Annie's thoughts. *Michael takes full responsibility by checking his communication skills if he is rejected. He doesn't beat himself up or criticise himself; instead, he has the awareness to know what he could improve on. Like Carla Buzasi, he has a strategy in place he can use, instead of crumbling in the face of setbacks.*

'There is a healthy version and an unhealthy version of an inner critic. Many successful people think it's the secret to their success as it can roust you out of bed and get you on that treadmill or spur you to finish that book, so they may achieve a lot, but they are totally miserable about it.'

Daniel F. Seidman, Columbia University Medical Centre clinical psychologist, Health Journal, 16 June 2009

Let's meet **Jamie**, who developed self-approval. Jamie is a good-looking 36-year-old guy who has a good job, a good salary and a good relationship with his family, and yet he has real issues believing that women will fancy him. If they don't show any interest at the first meeting, he immediately beats himself up. He is so focused on the approval of others that he doesn't have a clue what sort of woman he wants or the values he is looking for. His only aim is to be validated by someone finding him attractive, and then he thinks it will all fall into place.

We had several coaching sessions on influence, persuasion skills, assertiveness and communication techniques. Then I scripted several hypnotherapy sessions focusing on overcoming his low self-esteem and lack of self-confidence. We also worked on self-approval with some neurolinguistic programming (NLP) techniques to banish his inner critic and reframe his old limiting beliefs.

Jamie said:

I wanted to share this with Annie's readers because I honestly had no clue how I was behaving, and truly thought I had something inherently wrong with me. I felt so much anger that my friends were all in relationships and it just wasn't happening for me. I used the tools she gave me on colleagues and friends, not just women. However, when people started noticing a difference in me, my confidence started growing and I started watching how I would speak to myself, and then after three or four hypnotherapy sessions I felt a massive shift within. I can't explain it but it was totally amazing and I found myself speaking to women in a really easy, effortless way and not being bothered whether they responded to me or fancied me. I can't even put into words how grateful I am to Annie as I feel like a grown-up for the first time, like I am finally approving of myself.

Jamie's top tips. *Be aware of your habits by keeping a journal of your patterns of self-criticism and the need for approval. This highlights bad habits. Learn new communication skills and assertiveness techniques – get books on this or hire a coach – and things will change quite profoundly.*

Annie's thoughts. *Jamie is quite right, as the prerequisite for change is self-awareness and getting rid of old habits. Also, you need to learn how to become assertive and start communicating your needs so you can build self-approval.*

If you can find it within yourself to be compassionate and learn self-awareness by keeping a diary, carry on with it because it keeps you focused, helps you discover thoughts and feelings and even taps into your creativity.

Stop for a moment and reflect that perhaps you are as critical of yourself as your parents or teachers were of you when you were young. This can be a useful observation to help you find compassion for yourself and understand why you have this habit. Give yourself a mental hug and promise yourself to stop this nasty, cruel cycle right now.

Do not allow anyone to criticise you. They do it because they feel inadequate. If you get upset, critical people often say: 'I am only being honest.' In fact, they are being insulting and they get an emotional charge from dismembering others. When you have self-approval you will not believe them. You will brush it off and you won't react, because it is a reaction they are eager for.

The magic of mindfulness

Since 1970, modern clinical psychology and psychiatry have developed a number of therapeutic applications based on the concept of mindfulness, derived from Buddhism. There is no doubt that mindfulness has become 'hot' in counselling and health psychology. However, although some will immediately give it a try, many, more narrow-minded, people feel it's too 'out there'. Remember: successful people never knock things without having tried them first. This is what we call 'contempt prior to investigation'. Small-minded people are cynical, full of fear, lack confidence and need to be in control, so they will always mock and reject things they are unfamiliar with. So many judge others in today's world because deep down they are judgemental about themselves; they struggle to practise mindfulness, as it involves us experiencing what we feel without making a judgement. This is not a simple relaxation technique, it's not some new-age fad, and it is not a cure for all. Further information can be found on page 235.

This simple concept is the subject of plenty of legitimate research. It helped me reduce my anxiety, fear and stress, to stay focused, to heighten my self-awareness and to feel more tolerant towards myself and others, and it has helped many of my clients.

The US embraces it. In the US business world, interest in mindfulness continues to rise dramatically. Companies including those listed in the *Fortune* 500 state that executives who meditate consider the practice beneficial to running a corporation. Among them are Bill Ford, the chairman of Ford, and Michael Rennie, the managing partner of McKinsey and Company.

Harvard Law School holds workshops on mindfulness in the law and alternative dispute resolution. Many Los Angeles police officers receive mindfulness training, and it has been taught in many prisons, resulting in a reduction of mood disturbance and hostility. Clinics, the armed forces and hospitals around the US have also introduced it, as well as public and private schools in the greater Los Angeles area. Goldie

Hawn is in talks with the UK government to bring it to schools in this country.

Simple, powerful, effective

Mindfulness is about observing what happens and discovering who you are and what makes you tick. It's about exploring yourself without judging yourself. Often you form habits that become automatic and are based on adaptations of past events and situations; these are not helpful and often keep you stuck and repeating old habits even though your present situation is not identical to your past circumstances. You then stay trapped in that maladaptive reaction because of incorrect beliefs from your past, distorted perceptions and worn-out habits. It isn't possible to change these if you are not conscious of what you are doing; and you cannot be conscious of your unconscious choices.

You can only choose to perceive and respond differently once you are aware of your behaviour, and for this to happen you need clarity about where you are. When you are mindful, you bring about a reality that is effortless. You aren't attached to your thoughts. It's about trusting and going with the flow, as you never know what will emerge when you practise mindfulness. Your old habits do not disappear, but you create new ones; by practising mindfulness, you can interrupt old habits and learn to respond in a different way.

Mindfulness is really a simple concept in that it's about paying attention in a particular way. This entails being present in the moment and being non-judgemental about yourself or others. The result is heightened self-awareness, clarity and self-acceptance. Rather than reacting and allowing your buttons to be pressed, you become more aware of your thoughts, feelings and bodily sensations, and can then grant yourself the gift of choice and freedom from old limiting beliefs and habits that no longer serve you.

Mindfulness is often described as choosing and learning to control our focus of attention. If you have strong or loud thoughts, you can move attention to your breathing, your body or the sounds of your environment. Although at times your mind may be full of turbulence, anxiety and negativity, by practising mindfulness and learning to focus on your breathing you respond differently.

Observe yourself without judgement

Write down something about a specific time when you felt sad, ashamed, stressed, resentful or angry. For example, 'I felt ashamed when I put on a lot of weight,' or, 'I felt angry when X didn't return my telephone calls.' It doesn't matter how big or small the event was, just that it's a real occasion that left you with negative feelings. The important thing is to write about it without judging yourself and to ask yourself: 'What is going on for me at the moment?'

Simply allow yourself to observe whatever happens and what your thoughts are; just ask them nicely to float away, and turn your attention to your breathing or your surroundings. If you want to, you could label those thoughts and feelings – for example, 'that's an angry feeling' or 'that's a sad feeling' – and be aware that 'this too shall pass', that any intensity will decrease. The powerful part of this simple exercise is that you allow yourself to be an objective observer as opposed to someone who becomes disturbed by every feeling or thought that comes up. This does require practice, but is an amazing technique to use when you feel anxious or stressed. We all feel disappointed about some part of our lives – get over it.

Rules for staying in the moment

Everyone has the ability to become mindful by being in the present moment and disengaging from mental clutter. It's a very powerful thing to have a clear, decluttered mind as it means that you're focused, serene, sharper and much more alert, which will help you hugely in work or study, in creativity or romance. The mindfulness technique is not about concentration (although of course concentration is important as it helps us to focus our attention on one thing or another, and to take control of what's going on inside our mind).

It is aimed more at a state of awareness and a 'presence' of mind. Therefore, you can wave goodbye to your internal committee and their negative chattering, as mindfulness overrides their busyness. When you practise mindfulness, you are in the present moment and aware but not trying to control anything. Instead, you let everything organically pass by.

Guidelines for self-kindness

It's amazing that so many clients describe how cross they get with themselves if they don't hit their targets. It seems an epidemic in the 21st century for us to feel that if we don't push, push, push, we will lose our job or our partner, and we panic. Many punish themselves by not having enough sleep, feeding themselves fast food or not taking care of their needs or wants. Setting goals in any area of our life is good, but neglecting ourselves in the process is not.

It's extraordinary how mean many people are to themselves if they are not meeting their own unrealistic expectations. How would it be if you stopped when you had the urge to push, push, push even more and instead paused for a moment, asking yourself: 'What is it I need right now? Sleep, or a glass of water, a walk, a bath, or maybe a chat with someone I care about?'

I hear constant remarks from clients, friends and colleagues along the lines of:

- 'I am totally stupid.'
- 'What a complete idiot I am.'
- 'I can't believe how thick I am.'
- 'I can't remember anything.'
- 'I am just useless.'

Would you speak to your closest friends or your children that way? If not, why would you use such cruel words and such judgemental comments about yourself? Successful people praise and acknowledge themselves; they are cool about their imperfections. They don't try to be superheroes. Be aware that if you are unkind to yourself, you will subconsciously attract others to be unkind to you.

Please stop reprimanding yourself every time you get something wrong. On some level, being punished as a child leaves a lasting imprint, causing many of us to believe that we deserve to be punished. What is your reward for repeatedly being unkind to yourself? Do you do it from habit, or from truly believing that you are unworthy?

The power of pressing the pause button

Stop, breathe and pause, and monitor what you are saying to yourself. Self-criticism will always change your feelings, so keep a close eye on your inner critic whenever someone says something unkind, you make a mistake, you fail an exam or audition or don't get the job you have set your heart on, the guy you fancy doesn't ask you out, you don't get the contract you pitched for or your weight is not shifting as much as you had hoped on your new diet.

Remember to check whose voice are you hearing: your mum's or your teacher's or your ex's or the voice of someone else who used to condemn you? Ask your inner critic what it is trying to achieve. Question your judgements and keep asking your inner critic what its aim is. Not only will you challenge the inner voice, but you will also start changing those limiting beliefs you have been carrying around forever.

Take this new behaviour seriously, but take yourself lightly. If you usually tell yourself you are stupid for messing up, have a laugh and say to yourself: 'Oops, I did it again!'

Use a journal and record the triggers, beliefs and habits of your inner critic so you can master them. Highlighting worn-out behaviours is a great way to control them because awareness and knowledge are powerful. Once you master these, you will decrease their intensity, and spotting the patterns will reduce the frequency, so take a pad and make a note of them. Here is an example to help explain.

TRIGGERS, BELIEFS AND HABITS

The situation. I am furious that having sent out so many CVs I have only had one response for an interview.

Your inner critic. My teacher at school was right. I will never amount to anything. I am useless.

Your feelings and behaviours. I feel so frustrated I am not getting responses. I ought to give up any thought of applying for a management role. I will only ever stay in a junior position as I don't have the experience required. Who am I kidding, trying to move up?

But being positive. I got my first job in retail without any experience. I worked hard and was reliable and honest, so there's no reason someone won't take a chance on me in another company at a more senior level. I have good references and am presentable. Why shouldn't I be given a chance? After all, everyone has to start somewhere.

Annie says. OK, so if it hasn't actually happened what evidence or tangible proof do you have that you will be rejected?

'The bear is what we all wrestle with. Everybody has their bear in life. It is about conquering that bear and letting him go.'

Jennifer Lopez

Well said, J-Lo!

SUMMARY. WINNING THE BATTLE OF SELF-APPROVAL

- ◆ Believe that you have a place in the world, because you do. When you learn to like yourself, you will learn to approve of yourself. Find the person within yourself that you genuinely like and can become friends with.
- ◆ Discover yourself, and get excited about doing so as everything will change when you let go of the need for approval from others. Say to yourself over and over again 'I am worthy', 'I am more than enough'.
- ◆ Know you share equality with all humanity and you are just as good as anyone else. Translate that belief into self-approval.
- ◆ Stop succumbing to the way others perceive you. Push yourself to live the best life you can and give up self-criticism. Be considerate to yourself and keep a note of this by having a success journal. Record every single success — whatever the size.
- ◆ Check for misplaced and disguised anger. Identify your patterns.
- ◆ Give mindfulness a go.

A call to action

1. The lessons I have learned about self-approval are:

....

....

2. A person or situation I have needed self-approval around is:

....

....

3. I have looked to others for approval because:

....

....

4. The excuses I might make to avoid facing this realisation are:

....

....

5. The steps I will take to find self-approval are:

....

....

ANNIE'S CONFIDENCE-BOOSTERS FOR SELF-APPROVAL

◆ Set a boundary.
◆ Check yourself before automatically saying yes.
◆ Mind your own business.
◆ Stop justifying and defending your decisions.
◆ Remember that others' opinions are opinions, not facts.

Secret no. 3

SELF-ACCEPTANCE

Successful people are comfortable
being authentic

'You really have to look inside yourself and find your own
inner strength, and say: "I am proud of what I am and who
I am, and I am just going to be myself."'

Mariah Carey

The backbone of self-acceptance

Self-acceptance is a very important component of self-confidence.
Unless you accept yourself you can't have self-confidence. You need
to embrace yourself as you are right now, regardless of your past, your
mistakes or your weaknesses. A big misconception of self-acceptance
is that you need to like everything about yourself. That's not the case
here; we don't have to like everything about ourselves.

'I am not going to lose weight because others don't like
the way I look. I make music to be a musician, not to be
on the cover of Playboy.'

Adele

Self-acceptance does take some work, and yes I know I keep repeating
that you need to have self-awareness, but I want you to really grasp
this. You must step outside your comfort zone and separate who you
are from what you have done. There are things each of us excel at
that others would love to be able to do, so start acknowledging your

strengths. There could be parts of you that you disapprove of or dislike, but please don't trash these.

Meet **Anya**, who determined her own personal strength. Anya is a gorgeous 33-year-old, six-foot-tall, stylish woman. She is kind, witty, smart and works in the public sector. She takes care of her brother financially, and is a caring, considerate daughter, yet she doesn't accept herself. She criticises herself, puts herself down, has to be perfect as far as her clothes her body and her work are concerned, in all she does and says. She puts a huge amount of pressure on herself. Her parents wanted her to be a lawyer or a doctor, so in her eyes she is a failure and a disappointment to them.

From what she told me it was clear they wanted her to achieve these goals for their own gratification. She never had the nerve to tell her parents she has always dreamt of setting up a business. She therefore stays in a safe job she doesn't enjoy. I asked her if she was willing to share some mistakes she had made in her life with me and she agreed. By reading these out to me, she mastered her sense of shame and she ended up crying and laughing as she realised that I wasn't judging her. Yet she had been bound by shame for years.

Anya left her job and set up a business online, which is doing extremely well. She is much stronger as a person, and isn't concerned that her family does not approve.

Anya's success story:

Wow! Words cannot express what a huge relief it was to share my mess-ups and defects and not be criticised, lectured or judged. This was such a turning point in my life, as I realised I didn't really know myself and neither could I entirely accept myself until I shared what I felt shame about. I had been living with a constant fear of exposure, which is probably why I never let men get too close to me. I always felt a fraud, as though if you knew how much I had messed up, you would leave me. I felt understood by Annie. I did feel some regret and remorse, although I realise that a lot of what had happened, like having one-night stands or experimenting a few times with coke, or nicking £10 from mum's purse when I was a teenager, now seems blown out of proportion because I had kept it all to myself.

Anya's top tips. *Find a close friend you trust and share something you feel guilt or shame about. Strictly no feedback. I have no idea how it works, but it releases something deep inside and brings enormous self-acceptance.*

Annie's thoughts. *Toxic shame and guilt thrive in the dark, so when you bring them into the light, it takes away their power. It is crucial when sharing with someone that they do not criticise, or make remarks, but just accept what we say without judging us.*

Sharing your shames is very healing, and it means you can be who you are and not hide from yourself or others. Often you are controlled by things that you feel guilt about. Once you unconditionally accept your mistakes, you can start accepting yourself and learn that mistakes are what you do, not who you are.

Stop picking on yourself

Self-acceptance is an attitude and a way of looking at yourself and the world around you. It is a willingness to see things as they are without any judgement. Self-acceptance is an incredible state to achieve. Today, everyone strives for all or nothing, perfectionism, quick fixes and instant gratification, which stems from insecurity, low self-confidence and low self-esteem.

> 'Confidence is a kind of attitude. The most sexy people I know are the ones who have the guts to just be themselves. It's hard to find people like that in Hollywood.'
> John Cusack

You must not pick on yourself as this will erode your self-confidence. I will keep repeating that you must separate who you are from what you have done. Face your mistakes and learn from them; embrace what you think, feel and believe. Your feelings belong to you and they will stay within you until you deal with them, so get friendly with them and stop avoiding them.

Self-acceptance is an attitude that allows you to believe you are truly good enough. The external world is shaky, so if you lose your standing, you crash and lose your identity; if there aren't copious labels and awards bestowed on you, your confidence crumbles.

Self-acceptance is life-changing, and not possessing it is destructive and non-productive. It is essential to make friends with yourself. You may have met loads of people, but now it's time to genuinely meet yourself.

Quit comparing and despairing

Stop feeling you need to conform to be accepted by others. You are not bound by what they think of you. If you look to get everyone's approval you will wear yourself out, as it is a full-time job and completely futile. Find acceptance in yourself, and you will then feel positive and confident even when your expectations are not met.

If your parents didn't convey to you constantly that you were acceptable just as you were and that it was OK to make mistakes and get things wrong, then you may have viewed yourself ambivalently. You may have been hugged or rewarded only for getting things right or doing as you were told; this would imply that you were taught that only certain behaviours were acceptable and that you were shown conditional love. If this was the case, then growing up you would be programmed to see yourself as inadequate. Some of you may have suffered from mental abuse, being told by parents, teachers or carers that you were not smart enough, not thin enough, not fast enough. Often this may have been said in a jokey way, but whether it was said overtly or subtly, it would still have been unkind and damaging.

If this happened to you at school or at home, you may be excessively critical towards yourself and others. You do it unconsciously as it is familiar behaviour – you have learned to 'parent yourself' the way you were parented. If anyone ridiculed you or flagged up your defects in front of others and you were already lacking in self-confidence, it would have cemented your belief that indeed you were defective.

'It's OK if you mess up — give yourself a break.'

Billy Joel

Acknowledge your greatness

You have to get to a place of self-acceptance sooner rather than later and waste no more time believing this rubbish you were told. You are more than good enough just as you are. Firstly, you have to find some compassion for yourself, and secondly, you have to adopt a strong relationship with yourself to form a strong sense of identity. It's crucial you quit feeling you have to prove yourself to everyone to demonstrate your worth. Your aim is to like and respect yourself.

Conquering failure through self-acceptance

I talked to **Dr David Hamilton**, a scientist, international speaker and bestselling author of seven books. David was declared bankrupt in 2003; however, by adopting self-acceptance he started again and became even more successful than before.

David told me:

My family and the friends closest to me describe me as positive, busy and kind. My mum inspired me as she is the kindest person I've ever known and I learned from her that it's not so much what you do that counts, but the space within you that you do it from, and therefore have always admired those who are kind and gentle towards others. I get motivated by explaining stuff. Sounds daft, but it's kind of what I do. I write books and give talks, where I take what can be construed as complicated and simplify it so everyone can understand. I tend to meet the world in a very positive way and have complete self-acceptance. Even though I have overcome enormous setbacks, I still dared to live my dream. It was very challenging in 2003 when I went bankrupt after co-founding and running a charity for two years because I had to take several small jobs. However, through sheer determination to succeed and inspire others I focused all my efforts on writing my first book.

David's top tips. *Don't worry about rejection, just get on with things. Make your motto 'There's always a way'. When one door closes, another usually opens. Trust that everything always works out for the best in the end. Accept yourself and know you are worthy of success.*

Annie's thoughts. *David's self-acceptance is impressive. Many would have lost all confidence, but David got straight back up and started again.*

Easy does it

All your actions up until now have been compelled by a combination of your background and your biology. If you have acted badly towards others you ought to make amends, but you need to consider making amends internally for any harm you have done to yourself as well. Given your upbringing and programming by family, teachers and peers, it might have been pretty tricky to behave any differently. So please ease up on the self-flagellation for not being Mr or Ms Perfect!

Rediscover your true self

'The more you mature, the more you realise that your imperfections are what make you more beautiful.'

Beyoncé

So many clients and colleagues say:

- 'When I get the promotion I will be OK.'
- 'When I reach my target weight I will feel good about myself.'
- 'When I buy a Mercedes I will know I have made it.'

You are more than good enough exactly as you are. You won't give yourself real confidence, self-esteem and self-acceptance by having the big house, the degree, the rich boyfriend or girlfriend, the qualifications, the car. They are irrelevant to your self-worth – it's all a trap you have bought into. Self-acceptance is being OK with having shortcomings. Successful people work on themselves and keep moving forwards with their self-mastery. Virtually every client and colleague I speak to tells me what their weaknesses are and rarely tells me their strengths. Start off by telling yourself daily what your strengths are. You are human and that means you make mistakes; don't think for a second that that makes you odd, as every single person in the world has messed up more times that we will ever know. Start making changes today!

'It's much better to be yourself than to try to be some version of what you think the other person wants.'

Matt Damon

When you lack self-confidence you will constantly focus on the unrealistic expectations and standards of your parents, partners, peers, friends and work associates. By evaluating yourself independently, you avoid the constant inner turmoil that stems from relying on external opinions and views. Once you start accepting who you are and what you stand for and start to feel good about your talents, behaviour, work and beliefs, you will start owning your power rather than giving it away to everyone else and allowing them to control your internal and external world.

Exposing your attitude to yourself

When you react, or over-react, with an emotional charge to someone, you can be sure that person has uncovered your dark side, which needs healing by self-acceptance. Get friendly with your flaws as well as your assets and accept that, like everyone, you have a dark side and a light side. Accept yourself and refuse to lower your standards professionally or personally to live up to other people's ridiculous expectations. For example, when dating someone there is often an instant attraction or 'chemistry'; however, as a person with a strong sense of self and high self-confidence, you should be more cautious and want to know about the other person's sexual history, career, hopes, fears and values before giving yourself to them and before entering into a relationship.

Stop, look, listen

You would never buy a plot of land in a foreign country and then start building haphazardly. You would want to know you had a secure, strong foundation on which to build before parting with your money. Why wouldn't you do this in your relationships before parting with your heart? The same goes for friendships – slow down; you won't lose anything worthwhile or miss out if you don't respond when the other party wants you to. It's utterly dishonest to seduce anyone under false pretences and a complete waste of time and energy.

> 'I couldn't be with someone who uses manipulation to get what she wants as she isn't confident enough to just tell me.'
>
> John Mayer

Give up what you are for what you want to become

Self-acceptance is also about what you do for yourself. You can really only find self-acceptance by doing, not thinking. You must start worshipping yourself by being nice to yourself. If you abuse yourself by eating fast food, going without sleep, saying yes when you mean no or neglecting your own needs, you will never achieve self-acceptance.

If you develop this love for yourself, your confidence will shoot through the roof. It's good to look at qualities you like in others – kindness, humour, thoughtfulness, sensitivity, discipline, passion, motivation – and start cultivating those qualities in yourself.

Do not appease yourself – revere yourself

I asked **Kara Messina** some questions on self-acceptance. Kara is in her 20s and the creator of a new men's streetwear label called Y'OH. In 2012 she was approached by Adidas to collaborate on two projects: her own sneakers, and customising a project for the 2012 Olympics. Kara is on her way to being a huge name, mark my words...

Kara told me:

My mother, Rosalie, has had the greatest impact on my life. When everything seems utterly hopeless she never engages in drama and worry; she is always certain it will work out fine. Consequently, watching her making decisions in life, which caused her to go two steps backwards then 10 steps forwards, has given me the confidence to take risks. Without that I would be far less innovative in my thinking. I am motivated by the idea that my work could have an impact on culture. I admire people who demonstrate a genuine desire to support others without any expectations. I don't get hung up on rejection, because if I get turned down I trust it's because I need to be available for something else. I always knew I wanted to have an impact on the world by being a designer; although my short-term goals are changeable, my mission has always been the same. At times I felt I was an impostor; however, I overcame that by acknowledging the authenticity in my work and having self-acceptance.

Kara's top tips. *Always remember to take risks, accept yourself, know that you are more than enough, and always bear in mind that you can't please everyone.*

Annie's thoughts. *Kara has her sense of values straight and is clearly confident about where she is heading and who she is. This stems from self-acceptance.*

Wake your spirit

Discover the place inside yourself where nothing is impossible. Be bold enough to claim that which you deserve. When you are doing what you love for a living, your self-acceptance will grow. Working for loads of money but not liking what you are doing is betraying yourself. Respecting your time, respecting yourself, respecting others and letting them be who they are, and focusing on being who you are, are all empowering things. Successful people forgive themselves if they mess up – no drama, no self-pity. They don't walk around thinking about their own shortcomings or those of others.

Choose love and acceptance or fear and resentment – it's your call.

'The world will ask who you are, and if you do not know, the world will tell you.'

Carl Jung

> ### TAKE A TIP FROM THE PRESIDENT
>
> Barack H. Obama was sworn in on 20 January 2009 as the 44th president of the United States, the first ever African-American to hold the office of US Commander-in-Chief, and now he has been voted in for a second term. In the 2008 election, Obama won 53% of overall votes. Do you imagine that after the election Obama sat in a dark corner moping and feeling that he wasn't good enough because nearly 60 million votes were cast for his opponent? It might have been discussed, but I bet he got on with the job in hand and focused on the nearly 70 million votes he *did* receive, and I bet he's thinking the same thing now that he's in his second term in office. Focus on the positive!

'What America is looking for is authentic people who want to go into public service because they believe strongly in something, not because they want to be elected.'

Susan Sarandon

Name, claim and dump old habits

It's such a waste of time and energy to focus on what is going wrong and what you don't have. Remember: if you pay attention to something, it grows. You need to send your attention to where you want it to go and starve your negative thoughts until they die.

We all have a need to feel secure and valued. When others demonstrate that they are hearing and understanding you (even if they don't agree with you), it makes you feel valued and acknowledged. When you allow people to speak over you, talk down to you, shout at you, ridicule or interrupt you, it can distort your views about what makes you a worthwhile person.

Many employers want you to believe that their approval is a key factor in your self-worth. Many friends want you to follow their advice and bend yourself to their views without having listened properly to your needs. Unfortunately, many people allow others' opinions of them to shape their views and are swayed by someone's academic credentials or status. Many people I have met have a huge IQ but not an ounce of common sense.

All that glisters is not gold

Some people jump into a relationship because they are turned on by the other person's intelligence, but they don't take the time to find out whether this person is *emotionally* intelligent. Amazing people who have bundles of common sense can feel inferior because someone's academic qualifications are better than theirs. You are a person, not an accomplishment. So many people mistake material wealth, success, looks and academic achievements for self-worth. In 12 years of coaching, no client has ever asked to see my exam certificates; they pay me for real-life results, not test results.

Real value is not about looks or wealth. All the contributors in my book are successful, but each one was carefully chosen because I know they have integrity and they are humble and sincere. Your level of self-worth should be independent of what you own, how much you have accomplished, your weight or your IQ. Why? Simply because you are one of a kind, and by having self-acceptance you will know that substance is the name of the game. No matter how beautifully a gift is packaged, what matters is what is inside the wrapping.

'At some point you have to say: "Enough, I can't be perfect." You have got to love what's yours.'

Alicia Keys

Cultivating your own self-worth

I spent many years being seduced by sirens only to hit the rocks and to discover that they were disingenuous. At times my self-worth was so low and I had zero confidence, so I put anyone who was more intelligent or richer than me on a pedestal and trusted them. The sad thing was that I didn't realise I had huge talents and gifts inside myself because I'd never opened my own wrapping. I was convinced that anyone who was highly educated or from a wealthier family or better looking, was better than me, was really confident, was genuine and had integrity.

Being able to accept yourself lays the foundation for having confidence in your abilities. You can then take risks, and be in control of your life.

Having self-acceptance means you don't have to be 'good' or 'deserving', you just need to be 'you'.

'We are all stars and we all deserve to twinkle.'

Marilyn Monroe

Self-acceptance makes you less defensive, and more likely to take responsibility for your actions. You are more likely to make constructive changes when you are not busy berating yourself. Many addictions are fuelled in part by a self-critical component. Those who accept themselves are far less likely to abuse themselves with addictive behaviour. If you do not find self-acceptance, you will live in denial and repress everything, which is a painful state to be in. I know: I did that for years.

Every one of us is bombarded with ideas and unsolicited advice on how we ought to think, behave, look, feel and live, by friends, parents, society and the media, and we are told we run the risk of rejection if we don't conform. Who made up these rules about what you must do and say and think? Who governs your mind, body and soul, if not you? It is utter insanity to be like everyone else. How can you be authentic or happy if you are bending over backwards to be as you 'should' be to keep everyone else happy? You will *never* satisfy everyone. By trying to do so, you are effectively saying that your dreams, values, beliefs and visions are unimportant.

If you do this, you run the risk of losing your sense of self and remaining invisible, following everyone else's dreams, visions and goals and becoming bitter and resentful deep down or in constant denial. Neither situation is good and neither works – you end up repressing your resentments and hiding your anger, and for many this results in depression.

It is a situation created by your internal committee and your ego. Remember: the ego is about being superior or inferior – it swings both ways.

'I don't like myself. I am crazy about myself.'

Mae West

People respect you when you have self-acceptance and the courage to be yourself. Paradoxically, people are misguided in thinking that they will be rejected if they reveal their true selves. Why would you be happy to settle for a poor imitation of yourself, when you can be the real thing? After all, isn't the real thing always more valuable?

Authenticity is key

Successful people are authentic and that's what makes them engaging and powerful. When you accept yourself you do not need to convince the world that you are good, worthy and deserving.

Your actions and the choices you made have shaped your life today, but you certainly don't need to carry your past labels and mistakes in a transparent rucksack everywhere as if they define you. Being authentic means being true to yourself and honest about who you are, but you don't have to spill everything to everyone; there is a difference between being honest and being revealing.

Get real

- Are you honest with yourself and others?
- Are you true to yourself?
- Do you have integrity?
- Are you the real deal?

- Do you own your power?
- Do you align yourself to your core values?
- Are you transparent?
- Are you who you say you are?
- Are you acting in accordance with your beliefs?
- Are you in tune with yourself?
- Do you walk your talk?

'I think the most important thing for me is to be true to myself.'

Jay-Z

Make amends to yourself

Write to yourself, and make amends for every cruel word you have ever said to yourself, for all the times you have abused yourself, neglected yourself, and allowed others to speak down to you, speak over you, humiliate you or be unkind to you. Make amends for all the times you have made promises to yourself and let yourself down. Write down all the wrongs you have done to yourself that have plagued you for years. Bare your soul with someone you trust. If it feels too uncomfortable then fill the bath with warm water and light a candle, let it burn out and dissolve in the water and then say sorry to yourself. Then give yourself a hug and let go. Think about the following questions.

- What can you change?
- What can't you change?
- What are your needs and wants?
- What are your bottom lines?
- What are your beliefs?
- What are your skills?
- What are your talents?
- What are your strengths?
- What are your motives?

Fact. You can never attract authentic friends until you start being authentic.

Fact. You can't be confident until you are authentic.

SUMMARY. LEAPING INTO YOUR SELF-ACCEPTANCE ZONE

◆ Give yourself a break. It's draining and exhausting to battle constantly against yourself. Stop attacking and speaking down to yourself. It is so important to accept every part of yourself before you can make lasting changes. Make amends to yourself.

◆ Turmoil and inner anxiety will melt away once you change your focus from head to heart and let go of this crazy insistence that you are perfect. Start accepting that you are perfectly imperfect. Stop picking on yourself.

◆ Be happy with who you are right now and let go of the delusion that you can only accept yourself when this happens or that happens.

◆ Make an agreement with yourself that you will appreciate, validate, accept, respect, cherish, like and honour yourself from this moment on. Be gentle on yourself and make amends for how you have treated yourself and how you have allowed others to treat you.

◆ Authenticity is key, so give up being fake.

◆ Always remember that all that glisters is not gold. Don't be duped.

A call to action

1. The lessons I have learned about self-acceptance are:

....

....

2. A person or situation I have needed self-acceptance around is:

....

....

3. I have felt a need to be accepted because:

....

....

4. The excuses I might make to avoid facing my need to be accepted are:

....

....

5. The steps I will take to find self-acceptance are:

....

....

ANNIE'S CONFIDENCE-BOOSTERS FOR SELF-ACCEPTANCE

- ◆ Develop a clear sense of direction for your life.
- ◆ Take responsibility for your life.
- ◆ Remind yourself daily that your potential is unlimited.
- ◆ Focus on your talents and skills.
- ◆ Keep reminding yourself that you are perfectly imperfect.

Secret no. 4

SELF-MASTERY

Successful people trust themselves and their intuition

'I feel there are two people inside me — me and my intuition. If I go against her she will screw me every time, and if I follow her, we get along quite nicely.'

Kim Basinger

Embrace your inner voice

In this chapter, I want to help you reclaim your power and learn to practise self-mastery by stepping out of childhood belief systems that no longer serve you. When you become your own master, you become best friends with your inner voice and comfortable with being in charge of what you think, do and say. When you learn to trust yourself you develop inner security. You stand by your convictions in the face of adversity.

Now that you've started to understand from previous chapters the many reasons why you might not be able to trust your own judgements and why you shouldn't allow others to manipulate you, I will focus on the importance of self-mastery, which is an essential process.

Successful people understand that the power of self-mastery is determined by their attitude. They master their intuition because they know it profoundly directs the course of their life. Confidence helps you to trust your intuition, choices and opinions. You pay a high price for not listening to your intuition and it takes courage to find and trust that tiny, still voice inside. It has your best interests at heart. It is your confidant.

Throughout history, intuition has been a proven asset for successful people. For example, Steve Jobs, Oprah Winfrey, Simon Cowell, Conrad Hilton and Donald Trump have all publicly acknowledged how much they are guided by their intuition. Steve Jobs often reminded the employees at Apple to 'Have the courage to follow your heart and intuition; everything else is secondary.'

Discover your own truth

When you breathe deeply and stay focused, calm and detached from emotions, you can receive clear guidance. This may sound too simplistic to be effective, but I urge you to give it a go.

Our intuition is always present and available 24/7. It warns us when we are facing negative, risky situations and it makes us aware we are on the right track through small signs. It is your job to be conscious of what these signs are and watch out for them. If you start doubting your intuition, you will be stuck in fear, confusion and procrastination, and your life will become painful.

The messages you receive may seem totally illogical; this, coupled with a lack of confidence, is why many people do not trust them.

MY THREE SIGNS

Four years ago, I was invited to co-present at a launch. I accepted. A few months later my agent said a producer wanted to see me in Los Angeles the same week. He said he would also be securing other meetings around that date with TV companies. The launch and the LA trip clashed and my intuition said 'go to LA', but I try to keep my word once I make a commitment, so it felt uncomfortable to back out of the launch. That night I meditated, asking for clear guidance and three tangible signs within 72 hours.

Sign 1. The following morning I was on my way to a meeting and randomly bumped into someone I hadn't seen in five years. She said: 'So how is LA?' I said: 'I'm not based in LA; I'm in London.' She looked surprised and said: 'I was speaking to someone recently and I was sure they said you had gone to LA.'

Sign 2. The following day I had a meeting with a coach I hadn't met and the first thing he said was: 'Would you consider working on a retreat together in LA?'

Sign 3. The following day I was walking up the steps of my practice in Harley Street and in front of me I found a dollar bill. I called my agent and said: 'We're on.'

Then I called the PR company to apologise, but they apologised and said that the launch had been moved back three months and were surprised I hadn't been contacted. Had I passed up on LA and not known this, I would have been gutted. The power of intuition.

'Follow your instincts — that's where wisdom manifests itself.'

Oprah Winfrey

Opening up to a new philosophy

Channing Joseph reported in *The New York Times* in March 2012 that the US Navy has started a programme to investigate how members of the military can learn how to fine-tune and improve their intuition during combat and other missions. The Navy's scientists revealed that troops in Iraq and Afghanistan had reported an unexplained feeling of danger before encountering an enemy attack or before running into an improvised explosive device.

Research in cognitive psychology and neuroscience into human pattern recognition and decision-making suggests that there is a 'sixth sense' through which we can detect and act on unique patterns without consciously or intentionally analysing them. The US Navy expects future research to offer insights into the scientific basis of intuition, a concept that many tend to confuse with the supernatural. The term 'sixth sense' is evocative but risks conveying the idea that intuition is a psychic or paranormal phenomenon.

Basically, intuition is information stored in our subconscious mind and is too fast for the reasoning mind. If you practise meditation and fire the committee in your head, you can improve your concentration process and help further develop your intuition.

Tapping into your internal compass

Unfortunately, few of us have been encouraged to trust our intuition and we are taught to deny or disown our gut feelings, doing what others suggest instead. How crazy is that? How come you don't know what's best for you but others do? Obviously, I am not advocating that you ignore all professional advice, but you also need to learn to trust yourself and your inner voice, rather than running around saying to everyone else: 'Save me, fix me, you know better than me.' Your inner voice can reveal your mission in life – it can help when you don't know what career path you want to take, or it can help when you need support or knowledge about a subject in which you don't have experience or training, leading you to the best person to approach. If someone recommends an expert or a contact to you, keep an open mind about what they are saying, then go away and tap into your intuition. If they don't feel right for you, find someone else.

Keep tuning in to you

If you want self-confidence, remember your own opinion of yourself because it is worth a million times what others' opinions of you are worth.

It's the same in both your work and your personal life. If you are on a date and you get a hunch that something isn't right, even if the other person is charming, listen to that hunch. Just because someone is friendly, charming and kind doesn't mean they are trustworthy. Con artists can be friendly, charming and kind. Players can be witty, generous and polite. Untreated addicts can be sensitive, loving and compassionate. Many charmers are disingenuous. Some of my clients get defensive and don't want to hear the truth because it might mean that they have to end a relationship, job or partnership that they have had concerns about. Although they heard that niggling voice, they have chosen to ignore it, saying that they don't believe in this thing called 'intuition'. They trust only logic, but what they don't get is that their logic is forcing them to remain in a difficult situation.

If you have a gut feeling about a potential partner and you ignore it then it all goes wrong years later, it can be incredibly painful to face the fact that you spent many unhappy years with someone you had a bad feeling about from day one, but that you chose to ignore it. It's the same in business. I have lost a lot of money by going into business with partners I had initial concerns about; but because of my low confidence and lack of belief in my intuition I allowed them to charm me, and I invested time, energy and money in partnerships that later cost me dearly – in emotional, spiritual, financial and physical terms.

Everybody needs to approach others for guidance at times, and in fact the smartest, most successful people do this and delegate. The rational mind is infinite but can operate only on the experience you have had personally and have gained through your five senses. If you align logic, knowledge, feelings and intuition, you will always make powerful decisions.

A lifetime warranty

Logic and science, of course, have an excellent track record in that they have solved countless problems over the centuries, and your mind provides ready access to both intuitive and logical thinking. What people who are cynical about intuition do not grasp is that your intuition – seeing, feeling, hearing and knowing – drives you to make logical decisions. Socrates and Mozart both reported hearing an inner voice and following its advice. Thank goodness they did, as otherwise we wouldn't have enjoyed the gifts they brought us. In order to accomplish your goals, you need the help of your intuition to draw on your own personal power, and to bring clarity.

Every time you ignore your intuition and buy into someone else's negative opinions, you are reaffirming old childhood beliefs that others are right and you are wrong, that they are OK and you are not. You must never allow anyone to take away your passion and enthusiasm. So many people think intuition defies logic or that it's for people who are into spiritual beliefs. Your intellectual mind is strong, yet your intuition is way wiser and far more accurate. The aim of your intuition is to get past your intellect.

The power within

Dr Judith Orloff, one of the finest psychiatrists of our time, is assistant clinical professor at UCLA. Her work is featured on CNN, in *USA Today* and on *Oprah*, and her client list includes a host of Hollywood royalty. Her three books have been *New York Times* bestsellers. I asked Judith about the importance of intuition.

Dr Orloff told me:

My Daoist teacher has been the major influence on my writing, my career as a physician and my personal development as a spiritual being. Without a doubt the best advice anyone ever gave me way back was to trust myself. When people are mavericks, risk takers, courageous and walk through fear, I admire them, and even more so when they trust their intuition and don't sit in their heads. I also admire those who believe in kindness. As a creative, intuitive person, learning the basic sciences in medical training stretched my brain in ways it was never used before. I had to master linear logical thinking and all of the basic sciences to pass my courses and learn about the magical workings of the human body and brain. I found it very challenging to keep my centre and believe in myself and keep moving forward. Many people ask me if I was always clear on what I wanted to achieve, but no, not at all: my calling as an intuitive psychiatrist came to me in a dream and my intuition brought me guidance about what path to pursue.

Judith's top tips. *Trust in intuition, trust the moment, trust your inner voice and believe in a loving power greater than yourself that can guide your life.*

Annie's thoughts. *Judith is a wonderful example of someone who has the confidence to trust her inner voice while working in a profession that promotes linear logical thinking.*

Intuition has a quiet charisma

Your inner wisdom guides your thoughts, actions and decisions to help you be anything you want to be, to help you get to wherever you want to get. The more you listen to it and trust it, the louder and stronger it becomes. Are you prepared to let your intuition guide you, protect you, and direct you to a better place?

We all have intuition. However, successful people have the confidence to follow it in the face of adversity and trust it, which is one of the main reasons why they have become successful. Sometimes it comes from a hunch, a vision, an inspirational thought, a feeling deep in the pit of your stomach or a 'sixth sense'.

The potency of clarity

It never ceases to amaze me how few people know what it is they want to establish or what their needs are. So many clients tell me they have reached the top of the ladder in their career, only to realise that they are on the wrong ladder. So many tell me they stayed with a partner they were unhappy with for years as they didn't know what they needed or wanted and felt they were better with the devil they knew.

In order to learn self-mastery you must have goals and clarity. If you don't, you end up being blown around by the wind and living up to other people's expectations, meeting their needs and wants. Knowing that you want to get married, move home, make more money, have kids, start a business or travel is not the same as having goals, nor does it mean you have clarity. Having clarity means being specific and having definite goals, while being as clear as possible about the detail. The best way to predict the future is to create it. You are the only one who can decide what is best for you. When you lack confidence, people will try to manipulate you into their way of thinking. Only you have the answers and from those comes clarity. What others think of you and your goals and visions is irrelevant.

The force of determination

I spoke to **Sharon Wolter-Ferguson**, who was very clear about her vision. And she trusts her intuition. Sharon is founder of hardlyeverwornit.com, the first international online portal for buying and selling pre-owned luxury items. In less than six months, Sharon acquired an office in Monaco and then an office in the US to facilitate her VIP services. Sharon's clients include several Hollywood A-listers, and it has been reported that Kate Moss raves about the website.

Sharon told me:

My best friend, Amanda Thompson OBE, managing director of Blackpool Pleasure Beach, took over her family business on her father's early death and she employs over 2,000 staff in a tough business, so she really inspires me. It's so easy to give up when things get difficult, so I follow the best advice I was given, which is 'When you hit a hurdle, knock it down'. That's why I admire others who persevere, are optimistic and resilient, plus those who are kind and loyal. Like anyone, I don't like rejection; however, I deal with it very well as I have an optimistic nature. I had the courage to go from being a stay-at-home mum and throw myself into the tough world of business. I overcame any doubts by listening to my family and friends, who encouraged me to go for it. I am so motivated by wanting everyone to love hardly-everwornit.com as much as we do. Fortunately, I have always had sheer determination, and I think that's a big reason why I've been successful. Since I had the original idea for hardly-everwornit.com, I have been very clear about what I wanted it to become and it's so fulfilling to watch it happen.

Sharon's top tips. *My mantra to each and every one of you, which always makes me put back my shoulders and soldier on is: 'When you hit an obstacle, knock it down.'*

Annie's thoughts. *Firstly, Sharon took a brave leap, and, secondly, she trusted her intuition and was very clear about her vision.*

Are you going backwards, staying stuck or moving forwards?

You will only worry about what others think of you when you are not sure of yourself and your own thoughts, feelings, goals, visions and values. Your life, your path, your ideas, your thoughts, your beliefs and your evolution are your business; what others do is their business. You need to be clear about what matters to you: respect it, value it, hold it, and do *not* allow others to steer you off the path you have chosen.

You are always moving towards your goals or away from them. It is important to know what you want to accomplish, both personally and professionally. How can you hit a target if you cannot see it? In order to succeed in life you have to make a covenant with yourself that you will try to put into practice the things you feel will most benefit you. For every plan you make, you need to cover these five points.

1. What?
2. How?
3. Where?
4. When?
5. Who?

Write down your needs with regards to each of these points.

You often feel awkward admitting you need more money, more support, more respect, to be heard more or valued more or to be in a more rewarding job, or, if you are self-employed, to work more with a team rather than by yourself. However, having a heightened awareness and clarity will mean finding the ability to move forward.

Once you have written down your personal or professional needs, explore them to see whether there are needs that keep appearing. Many clients tell me they are not getting their needs met by their partner or their bosses, siblings, business partners or friends, and yet when I ask if they communicate this, they say they feel embarrassed or uncomfortable. You have to be specific, tune into yourself and trust your intuition when it informs you that you have unmet needs – you can't ignore them any longer if you want a happy and fulfilling life. Unmet needs can make people angry and resentful. By discovering your needs, you will become more proactive and feel much more empowered, which in turn raises your self-esteem and confidence. Firstly, be clear about which needs are not being met; secondly, ask. Effective communication skills help hugely. We will cover those in the next chapter.

Successful people have self-mastery and are crystal-clear about their purpose. Ask yourself which parts of your life give you most happiness and which cause most of your unhappiness. Write it down and get this clear, because it's important you realise that clarity doesn't just appear from nowhere; you have to decide for yourself what it is. If you are spending time with people who have no direction in life and just constantly 'go with the flow', they will not exactly inspire you to find clarity. Complaining, moaning and whingeing about what you haven't got and what's going wrong won't bring clarity either. Lack of sleep, too much coffee, excess alcohol, too much sugar, wasting time on video games and TV won't bring you clarity. Maybe you learned at school, college or university how important clarity was and how crucial it was to know your values and have your needs met … but I doubt it, so take note now.

The desire behind the action

I asked **Denise Robertson** MBE to answer a few questions on self-mastery. Denise is the author of 18 books, a national treasure and the resident agony aunt on ITV's *This Morning*.

Denise told me:

Pope John XXIII really inspired me when I saw the newsreel of him visiting a prison, and showing such love towards such awful criminals that it made me feel ashamed of getting angry with people. I guess I believe in self-mastery and am motivated by the excitement of what may happen tomorrow. I was once given a wonderful piece of advice, which I follow always: don't stare down the future, it will scare you; make sure you live in the moment. That works for me, coupled with the fact I don't have an issue with rejection as I simply accept it and move on, which is what I have always done. I therefore admire others who are determined, even more so when they are compassionate and have a sense of humour. These traits have certainly contributed to my success as I found it so challenging to be working away from home and my children. To be honest, in the early days it was about me supporting my own needs, because if I hadn't needed to work and generate an income for my family I simply wouldn't have done it. The desire to feed and support my children was what drove me and was what got me on that train.

Denise's top tips. *Live one day at a time and always remember it is crucial to never give up, to always keep going regardless of challenges.*

Annie's thoughts. *Denise was clear about her needs and crystal-clear about her goals, which she used as her driving force.*

Transform your life with discipline

Successful people are disciplined. They sacrifice their social life for a few months to achieve a goal, get up two hours earlier each morning to get to the gym, or say 'No' to cake when they want to lose weight. They make decisions about what behaviour best reflects their goals and values and many even have a mission statement. This is why I keep repeating how crucial it is for you to know yourself. Self-knowledge is powerful: without it you cannot know who you are and where you want to head. You have to be awake; you have to know what is working in your life and what isn't.

'Know thyself.'

Socrates

Discipline means having perseverance and restraint. It is a form of self-control. Successful people keep their eye on the goal at all times and do not veer off in other directions. They know too well that this will result in chaos. Like everyone else, each day they have stacks of ideas, impulses, requests, desires and demands competing for their attention. However, they are focused and do not waste time or effort being seduced by temptations, quick fixes or hits. They see the bigger picture and fixate on their dream. They have taken time to cultivate discipline.

Train your mind

Discipline displays inner strength and self-belief and it's very attractive. Successful people often have to postpone or eliminate any activities that will get in the way of their goal. Tricky circumstances and obstacles crop up persistently for all of us, but successful people do not allow themselves to be tempted or derailed. They are on a mission, which is to achieve what they want to achieve. This isn't just about business; the principle applies to absolutely anything. If successful people find that their old ideas and old thoughts haven't brought results, they get shot of them and propel themselves into a new state of consciousness by waking up to themselves and reframing the way they think and act.

'Attitude is a little thing that makes a huge difference.'
Sir Winston Churchill

You can do it!

If successful people say they are going to an event and will not drink as they have an early start the next day, they will stick with that decision. If they say they want to lose weight by a certain time and there's a party in the middle of their schedule with copious amounts of food on offer, they stay true to their commitment to themselves. That's why they are successful. The following day they feel good as they are on track – even if they may have fancied a few champagne cocktails, or a slab of birthday cake, their discipline ensures that they won't deviate from their goal. They will not falsify themselves to do what they think will please someone else.

Discipline requires practice and effort to achieve. It eliminates procrastination and indecisiveness. It is a skill I highly recommend you master to help change habits and behaviours, as you will see startling results appear and your self-confidence will increase profoundly. It doesn't matter how much talent you have or how smart you are, if you do not have discipline you will not achieve very much, you will plod along, and that results in a mediocre life full of negative habits, bent over in fear. It isn't a good look.

Replicate the positive habits of successful people

Successful people do not waste their precious time gossiping, thinking negatively or deliberating; they know this is a deflection. Successful people know there will always be temptations put in their path, but they also know that being disciplined means honouring themselves. They programme themselves to expect success and their sense of purpose is strong – they know they have to train their mind and they understand only too well that self-analysis and vigorous honesty are essential to hone these skills. They know they can't have the perk without the work. They know they have to say 'No' at times to things they want but don't need. They know the cost of success is discipline, and by thinking first and acting afterwards they develop self-mastery.

Successful people spend time with people who are proactive, confident and focused and whose goals and values are aligned with theirs. Do you? If not, consider hiring a business or personal development coach, a mentor, a fitness trainer or a counsellor, but don't give your power away to them. If money is an issue, check out colleges or offer to do something in exchange.

Defining your values

You can't expect to find clarity without knowing your values and knowing what is important to you.

You may already have a list of values, and, if so, I encourage you to do another list, because values can change as priorities change. The clearer you are about your values, the more you will gain clarity and focus on what is most important to you right now. So many people gloss over the fact that time is a limited resource; once you have spent it, it is gone forever. If you fritter away time and energy in actions that do not produce the results you want or take you away from your goals, you will not be happy, nor successful.

You may intend to stay on track but then become easily distracted by others, veering away from your goals and needs to end up resentful and angry, especially if you drift into places that don't fulfil you. If you are clear about your values, they will act as a compass by which you can navigate to where you want to be. It may be important for you to have good health, to devote more time to your family, or to open your own business, or perhaps it is a priority to have more leisure time. Whatever it is, you need to prioritise whatever is most important to you at this moment.

Your values are your standards, the qualities you consider important, and they vary for us all. They affect your life and help you focus on where and when you are willing to make sacrifices. If you set goals that go against your values, it will take forever to achieve them, so you need to set goals that align with your values. This allows you to work with energy, passion and vitality.

Ask yourself what is really important to you. I have listed some important values below, but there are literally hundreds more – feel free to add ones I haven't included. Tick off the 10 values that fit you best. Do not analyse: practise intuition here and go from your heart and your first feeling.

Acceptance	Balance
Accuracy	Boldness
Achievement	Brilliance
Affection	Calmness
Approval	Certainty
Attractiveness	Cleanliness
Awareness	Community

Confidence
Consistency
Control
Courage
Creativity
Determination
Dignity
Directness
Discipline
Diversity
Emotional sobriety
Empathy
Enthusiasm
Excitement
Expertise
Family
Faith
Fearlessness
Fidelity
Financial security
Flexibility
Freedom
Fun
Generosity
Gratitude
Growth
Honesty
Humility
Independence
Integrity
Intellect

Intelligence
Intimacy
Intuition
Justice
Kindness
Knowledge
Logic
Love
Loyalty
Making a difference in the
world
Marriage
Mastery
Motivation
Open-mindedness
Passion
Patience
Persistence
Pragmatism
Professionalism
Responsibility
Self-respect
Sensuality
Serenity
Sincerity
Sound emotional control
Strength
Thoughtfulness
Trust
Truth
Wealth

Connecting to your values

I suggest you prioritise your values: work down your selection of 10 and decide which is top, then second, and so on. Is marriage more important to you today than making loads of money, or is being motivated more important than having a spotless home?

Remember: these values are not set in stone, although you can have core values that remain the same, such as honesty, loyalty and integrity. You can revise this list from time to time to check your priorities and whether you're staying on track. If you are being true to your values – like all confident, successful people – you will focus on your top three above all else. Whichever values you have in your list, they are indeed important to you. Having clear values allows you to make decisions that work in your favour.

You don't have to live by the same values you have always had or ones you have inherited from your schooling or your family. Being aware of this will be helpful to your growth. The values that would make us millionaires or keep us toned and fit won't necessarily help you find your soul mate, so it is good to check on them periodically. Ensure that you know yourself better so you are not trying to meet everyone else's demands.

I have always found **Michael Neill** to be connected to his values and to follow the path of self-mastery, so I asked him a few questions. Michael is an internationally renowned coach and author of 12 books. Based in Los Angeles, Michael is mentor to many Hollywood stars. Paul McKenna describes him as 'the finest success coach in the world today'.

Michael told me:

My dad was a quiet inspiration. He was a good husband, a great father and an honest, caring and successful businessman. It wasn't until I was older that I realised not everyone was like that. Who knew that showing up on time and doing what you said you would was going to turn out to be a competitive advantage in life? I love spending time with people who love what they do, and I also admire people who can go up and talk to complete strangers without awkwardness. My son can do that, and I think it's amazing. If I get rejected, I find curling up in a little ball on the floor and crying works wonders. Then I get back up, move forward, and never give it another thought. Overcoming my own moods has been my most difficult challenge. I was a depressed, suicidal teen, and while it would be cool to say I overcame it through courage or persistence, I think the truth is I overcame it via grace. I had a moment of real clarity while I was in the middle of the worst of it, and I realised that despite the fact that I thought about it all the time, I didn't really want to die. After that, 'the suicide thought' stopped being scary — just a sign that I was feeling a bit overwhelmed. One of my core values is to be ... I'm not sure what the correct word is, but I'll go with 'agendalessness'. I really don't do anything with an ulterior motive — if I want to do it I will; if I don't want to do it, I won't. Consequently people know that they can rely on the fact that what they see is what they get. Some of my other values are honesty, integrity and kindness.

Michael's top tips. *Listen to advice but always follow your gut. There are three ways of doing anything — the right way, the wrong way and your way. Always do it your way. Worst case, you'll have a wonderful life. Best case, you'll have a wonderful life and drive a Porsche.*

Annie's thoughts. *Michael is clear about his values, knows his strengths and weaknesses, and strengthens his self-belief by trusting his instincts. And by developing self-mastery.*

> ## SUMMARY. MASTERING YOUR LIFE
>
> ◆ Master your life and master your emotions. Know your purpose, be courageous, get friendly with your values and connect to them. Practise self-discipline and focus so you do things in a deliberate and honourable way.
> ◆ Start by having a vision and set short-term and long-term goals. Focus on taking small, positive steps towards your goals each day. Remember that self-sabotage is a cruel way to stop yourself maximising your potential.
> ◆ When you get into negative thinking, write it down; next to this, write your emotions and list all the evidence that refutes the negativity. Then list some objective thoughts alongside. Always remember the power of aligning logic, feelings and intuition.

A call to action

1. The lessons I have learned about self-mastery are:

....

....

2. A person or situation I have needed self-mastery around is:

....

....

3. I would like to have self-mastery in my life because:

....

....

4. The excuses I might make to avoid facing the need for self-mastery are:

....

....

5. The steps I will take to find self-mastery are:

....

....

ANNIE'S CONFIDENCE-BOOSTERS FOR SELF-MASTERY

◆ Listen to your inner voice.
◆ Remind yourself – if they can do it, I can do it.
◆ Identify your strengths and weaknesses.
◆ Challenge all negative assumptions.
◆ Control your thoughts.

Secret no. 5

SELF-BELIEF

Successful people keep their
expectations high

---

*'When classmates "mentally bullied" me at school, I would
just sit there and think, "let this make you stronger".'*
Kate Winslet

Why is self-belief so important?

Self-belief is the main pillar of success. Confident people have indestructible self-belief. Many successful people had to build self-confidence as they went along. If you live by limiting beliefs, you will keep your world small and safe. Is that using your innate strengths and assets to the fullest of your potential? No way. It is living in fear and self-imposed limitation. If you believe you will fail, your subconscious mind will gather evidence to support that. Do you imagine that successful people have just had self-belief dropped into their lap?

When you have self-belief, you don't allow others to distort your perceptions. Each one of you is responsible for your experiences and you cannot allow others to tell you how you feel, nor can you allow what has happened in your past to keep controlling your present and your future.

Never, ever quit

Ronit Zilkha graduated with a BA in fashion design. She was hailed as the designer who revolutionised the British working woman's wardrobe in the 1990s. From catwalk to boardroom, her clothes became staples of celebrities in the UK and US, such as Julia Roberts, Kate Winslet, Cate Blanchett and Geri Halliwell, and even Princess Diana. Cherie Blair wore a Ronit Zilkha dress to enter Downing Street. In 1996, Ronit Zilkha Ltd was put into receivership as a result of bad advice, then in 2007 the company which owned her label went bust. In 2009, Ronit started from scratch again and now has a successful range of women's wear and children's clothes called Lullilu.

Ronit told me:

My daughter is and always has been my inspiration, because through raising a child and teaching them about life you have to listen to yourself. So when you say give it another go and don't give up, you are kind of saying it to yourself too ... You want them to see that you are practising what you preach and you want to set them the best example you can about life and living. I love it when my customers come back to me with comments like: 'I've been looking for a dress like this for what seems like half my life.' Many people still tell me how their Ronit Zilkha clothes are the most treasured in their wardrobe — that will always inspire me and spur me on. I really admire people who are honest, loyal and sincere and, like myself, do not get hung up or give up when rejected. It's all about self-belief and moving on and letting it go over your head. Like a lot of parents working, it is challenging to try to do it all, and working hard and raising a child is difficult at times. However, I plan and I organise and I focus on setting realistic targets that I can manage and finish in time instead of being swamped with endless tasks which I know will be impossible to achieve on time. I am doing the work I love, because since I was very young I always knew I wanted to be a fashion designer, and I think I have achieved more than I ever dreamed I would. I wasn't actually aware of my achievements until others told me, because, to be honest, I am driven by my passion to create something special for someone, and if I achieve that then I have achieved success.

Ronit's top tips. *My own mantra is: 'Don't look back ... look forward.' Be strong when everything seems to be going wrong and believe that tomorrow is another day. Believe in miracles.*

Annie's thoughts. *Ronit's self-belief is incredible. She has overcome enormous challenges and kept going. An inspiration to us all.*

'I've often felt unattractive or different looking. As I have grown up, I have felt more comfortable in my own skin. It may sound a cliché, but when you feel beautiful and strong on the inside, it shows on the outside.'

Angelina Jolie

Dare to live your dreams

It's pointless not believing in yourself – how can you decide something won't happen when you haven't yet tried it? If you have and it went wrong, try a different approach.

Confident, successful people do not quit or collapse at the first sign of trouble; they keep going and they don't make statements such as 'that isn't possible'. They keep their eyes open for whatever route they need to take to get to where they want to be. Keep remembering what is good about you. You do not have to be good at everything. The key is to stay positive and keep asking yourself how personally committed you are to making changes.

Successful people don't waste time listening to negative, insecure people. Only listen to those who:

- have what you want
- are experts in their field and can help you move forward
- champion and support your visions, dreams and goals
- have been exactly where you are and kept going through adversity.

'I am the girl who everyone said was never going anywhere. I guess I shocked a few people.'

Cher

Successful people make their happiness and their success a priority. People without confidence do not acknowledge their freedom of choice. It is your life and it's down to you to create what you want, regardless of your upbringing.

It is so easy to blame the economy, the government, your boss, the cost of living, the property prices and everyone else for our reluctance to change. The bottom line is that you are the only one who can change your situation. If you continue to live unconsciously and believe you are the victim of circumstances, absolutely nothing will ever change.

Discovering my inner strength from my father

My father achieved success, even though he had little education, no role models, no support, no family money, and no-one to champion him. Born in the East End of London with two brothers and a sister, for a period of time, for whatever reason, his mother put him and one of his brothers into an orphanage.

Did we ever hear him complain about what a bad mother he had, what a terrible childhood he had and how he'd suffered? Never once. He was absolutely not into 'poor me'. He inherited the wonderful strength of spirit of the East End, a steely determination, a strong-minded attitude, a 'get on with it' approach, a wise mind and a fair, big-hearted and grounded persona. My father believed we each had to be responsible for our life and no-one owed us a living. He drummed it into us that we couldn't strut about with a sense of entitlement or take anything for granted. He also taught us there was no such thing as 'can't'. He truly believed that if you put your mind to something and took action, you could make it happen; but you needed to be focused and be tenacious.

My father told me to go for it, keep my standards high, get back on track when I got knocked down, and let every setback strengthen me, not weaken me. Never listen to anyone who told me that I couldn't do something. Take an informed risk, aim high, and reach for the stars.

Put principles before personalities

My father taught me great principles – be polite, be respectful, be kind, be grateful, be honest, and have integrity and morals. These principles were drummed into us, and shaped us into the decent human beings we are today. We always had all we needed but we were not spoilt, and were taught to understand the value of money and hard work.

My father had a serious car accident when I was around 12 or 13 years old, and he was in hospital for a considerable amount of time. The internal and external damage was extensive and surgeons had to remove healthy skin from parts of his body and spread it over the affected areas. Later, they discovered he had gangrene in his leg, which was so severe they had to amputate it. We didn't know if my father would survive. We were all confused and scared. My father clearly made a subconscious and conscious decision to pull through and get back on track. He never sought attention, never regarded himself as a victim or took his upset or pain out on anyone else, and I figure he had a lot of upset and hurt inside – after all, a lorry had driven into him and driven off.

My father was told he wouldn't be able to walk again for a long time because it would be too painful, but he practised and practised, and although it was painful he was walking in no time. He didn't buy into statistics, obstacles and other people's limiting beliefs.

Ten years later, my father got back into a more secure place financially. My sister had married and my first nephew was born, and so he was enjoying being a grandfather and life was good. I was going to meet him for lunch when I randomly bumped into my brother, who had been trying to get hold of me to tell me our father had suffered a heart attack and died within minutes.

My life fell apart at that moment, and I felt such rage about him being taken at 59 years old. We found out at his funeral that he had secretly visited many hospitals and rehabilitation centres, motivating and supporting other amputees to have self-belief. I honestly have never come across anyone else with so much self-belief, such a big heart, and who gave as unconditionally as my father.

Annie's thoughts. *My father took a negative, painful situation and used it to demonstrate to us that we should not give up, not sit in self-pity. He blankly refused to allow negative situations to beat him. He could easily have been overwhelmed by his problems and made our life miserable, but instead he chose to face up to the solution. Even when he couldn't see a way out, at times he suspended his judgement and had faith. Having self-belief that you can find a solution to your challenges is the key. Having self-belief helps overcome adversity.*

'Some of the most devastating things that happen to you will teach you the most.'

Ellen DeGeneres

Determination, positive thinking and blind faith

So, don't tell me it isn't possible to overcome setbacks and pain. There are many people who live with severe challenges and yet have relentless self-belief. Just watching the Pride of Britain Awards every year makes me cry, seeing so many incredible children with such severe disabilities behaving so positively. They remind me of my father, who saw the positive in everything.

Remember: nothing will change until you change. As your self-belief deepens, you will start feeling you deserve to be happy and successful, allowing change to happen and understanding that it's not selfish to want to raise the bar and improve your life.

Change your perception

'I cried because I had no shoes until I saw someone with no feet.'

Persian proverb

Remember that self-belief is a learned behaviour. When you hear that doubting voice creep in, telling you that you are not smart enough, thin enough, rich enough, funny enough, tall enough, fit enough, experienced enough … think for a moment. Whose voice is it? You were not born with those thoughts or beliefs, so where did they come from? An ex-partner, a parent, a teacher, a bully at school or work, a sibling, a colleague, a boss or a business partner? Or are they from a mix of people over the years? Your lack of self-belief is based on perception, not reality.

Perception, not reality

It's so important to understand that no matter what is going on in your life or what isn't, it's your interpretation of the situation that matters, not anyone else's. Your interpretation and perception belong to you. Please read this a few times. Successful, confident people understand that reality doesn't exist in the abstract: it is all about perception.

You may have been taught from an early age to look to others for approval. Maybe you were punished if you didn't conform and others were rewarded for conformity. Sadly, many employees who come up with amazing ideas that might make the boss look bad get demoted, ignored or treated unfairly, whereas often the employees who say yes to everything are promoted. This knocks confidence and self-belief.

Overcoming setbacks

However, as I have said, many famous people suffered such experiences and it didn't stop any of them following their dreams, so you can't use bad memories as excuses. Walt Disney, Thomas Edison, George Bernard Shaw, George Eastman (inventor of the Kodak camera), Albert Einstein and Quentin Tarantino didn't do well at school, while Avril Lavigne and Hilary Swank both quit.

> 'Just be confident in what you know for yourself. You will have pressures from different people who will try to tell you that they know what's best for you. We all know, deep down inside, that inner voice ... those dreams that we have that people are constantly telling us that we can't achieve ... we know we can.'
>
> Jada Pinkett Smith

THREE MOGULS WITH NO DEGREE

- **Lee Bollinger,** President of Columbia University, was rejected by Harvard: 'My experience cemented my self-belief that it was up to me alone to define my talents and potential. Don't allow rejections to control your life; to allow other people's assessment of you to determine you is a very big mistake. The question really is, who at the end of the day is going to determine what your talents are, and what your interests are? That has to be you.'
- **Ted Turner,** the $2 billion media mogul, was rejected by Princeton and Harvard: 'I want to be sure to make this point: I did everything I did without a college degree.'

- **Warren Buffet,** business magnate, investor and philanthropist, is worth $44 billion but was rejected by Harvard: 'The Harvard rejection prompted me to settle down and stop partying. The initial stumble was critical in getting me launched. The truth is that everything that has happened in my life ... that I thought was a crushing event at the time has turned out for the better. Setbacks teach lessons that carry you along. You learn that a temporary defeat is not a permanent one. In the end it can be an opportunity.'

'Every single negative can lead to a positive. Any negative situation ... don't get too down about it — you will work it out. You learn it as you go along. It will happen over time and it's the getting there which will be the most fun.'

Simon Cowell

I talked about self-belief to **Sue Stockdale,** who represented Scotland at athletics and became the first British woman to ski to the magnetic North Pole, and now inspires many through her motivational talks and books. She told me:

I was inspired by Robert Swan — the first man to walk to both the North and the South Pole. But I had never imagined similar sorts of successes were possible. Helping others to believe that they can do anything, too, motivates me, and I am also motivated by seeing people who are willing to step out of their comfort zone to try new things, like myself, and who possess self-belief. I admire those who are authentic and have the ability to be themselves, and I admire those who possess humility — to be modest and respectful and accept that they can still learn more. Rejection has made me stronger. I pick myself up and use the rejection as a motivator to prove to others I can do it — whatever 'it' is.

Sue's top tips. *When you are frightened to do something, ask yourself, what is the worst that can happen? And if you can accept the answer, then take the action! Self-belief and committing to action are key.*

Annie's thoughts. *Sue takes action to diffuse fear and makes a commitment to herself to see things through.*

Unleash your potential

The first place to start is to accept who you are and embrace your strengths. Be clear about what you do well and what you don't do so well. Get honest with yourself. This is no time to mess around — you want to see changes, right? You need to change the way you think and alter your perceptions. Change can come from inspiration or from desperation, but either way you have to want it.

Many people have suffered traumatic events and constant setbacks, and yet their interpretation of these events is what has made the difference between failure and success. It is never what has happened to you that defines you, it is how you choose to be as a result of those events and what you choose to focus on as a consequence.

NO-ONE SAID LIFE WAS EASY OR FAIR

- **Rudyard Kipling.** The youngest writer ever to receive a Nobel Prize for Literature was told 'I am sorry Mr Kipling, but you just don't know how to use the English language,' by the editor of the *San Francisco Examiner* in 1889.

- **Roger Bannister CBE.** Doctors and scientists said the four-minute mile was impossible, but Roger Bannister's self-belief endured thousands of monotonous laps to prove them wrong. To date, 955 runners have achieved the impossible dream, accomplishing the feat more than 4,700 times between them. 'Man cannot run a mile in less than four minutes! They would die in this foolish attempt. It is an impossible dream,' the BBC declared on 6 May 1954, the day Bannister achieved the record.
- **Oprah Winfrey.** Oprah endured a tough, abusive childhood and several setbacks in her career. She was fired from her job as a TV reporter because she was told she was 'unfit for TV'. Through her self-belief, she has become one of the richest women in the world and says: 'Failure is another stepping stone to greatness' (*LA Times*, 31 March 2012).
- **Jack Canfield and Mark Victor Hansen.** *Chicken Soup for the Soul* was rejected 140 times. Their series of books went on to sell over 100 million copies in 37 languages (Dennis Hughes, *Share Guide*, 2004).
- **Margaret Mitchell.** *Gone with the Wind* was rejected 38 times before it was published. It went on to win the Pulitzer Prize, and the film garnered eight Academy Awards.
- **Agatha Christie.** It took four years and more than 20 rejections before Agatha's first book was finally published (http://cristianmihai.net, May 2012).
- **Richard Bach.** *Jonathan Livingston Seagull* was rejected by 18 publishers. Macmillan picked it up and it sold over a million copies.
- **Stephen King.** His first book, *Carrie*, was rejected 30 times (www.examiner.com, March 2009).

- **J. K. Rowling.** Before her first book was published, J. K. Rowling was broke, depressed, divorced and trying to raise a child on her own while receiving benefits and writing her novel. *Harry Potter* was turned down by 12 publishers, including Transworld and HarperCollins. After being refused by a dozen agents, she was taken on by Christopher Little, who persisted in submitting the book for a year while an endless stream of rejections arrived at his door.
- **Michael Jordan.** The best basketball player of all time was dropped by his high school basketball team. 'I have missed more than 9,000 shots in my career. I have lost 300 games. On 26 occasions I have been entrusted to take the game-winning shot, and missed. I have failed over and over and over again in my life. And that is why I succeed.' (www.michaeljordanquotes.org, March 2012.)
- **Mia Hamm.** Mia is a legendary sportswoman and has scored more goals internationally than any other football player – male or female – in the history of the game. But she was born with a club foot and spent years in casts. Nevertheless, she dominates women's football and was chosen as one of FIFA's best players by Pelé (realwomeninsports.com, June 2012).
- **Orlando Bloom.** Film star Orlando has a major language-based learning disability. 'I encourage kids to never give up on their dreams, take obstacles and make them the reason to have a big life.' (www.communitybright-starlearning.com)

You can read more about some of these examples, and many others, at www.onehundredrejections.com.

I have had more comebacks than Tom Jones, and so I know only too well that self-belief is about overcoming setbacks, obstacles and rejection. Taking small steps brings big results, so be courageous and ask yourself: 'What is the worst that can happen if it goes wrong?'

Tap into your hidden strengths

When you tap into your hidden strengths, you will make smart choices, trusting they are the right ones for you and letting go of others' expectations of you. When you worry about others' expectations, you don't trust yourself to make the right decision, so you make the wrong decisions for the wrong reasons.

'Belief in one's self and knowing who you are — that's the foundation for everything great.'

Jay-Z

Many people don't make decisions: they avoid making a commitment so that they don't have to handle more responsibility or more success, or face others' disapproval. Often, people look to others to make the decision, so if it all goes wrong they don't look like a fool. You worry that your decision may offend or upset your boss, partner, sibling, colleague, neighbour, mentor or clients. If you win, they will lose, and so you justify your position by saying to yourself that you would be selfish if you made this decision. When you possess self-belief, you trust that the decisions you make are the right decisions. If it's a personal decision you need to make, and you are coming from a place of love, integrity and honesty, then it's always the right decision. Stop trying to be someone else.

'The most important thing in life is to live with integrity and not give in to peer pressure, to try to be someone you are not.'

Ellen DeGeneres

If it's a professional decision and you feel intimidated because you don't have enough information, go and find more and buy time to investigate. Take responsibility for making a smart decision. Those lacking in confidence pass the decision on to someone else, and then if things go wrong they blame that person. Those with self-belief determine what skills they require, who they can speak to for more information, and use this to make an informed decision — and they trust their intuition. Practise with small decisions and take it a day at a time; when you start achieving results by trusting your intuition and increasing your self-belief, you can move on to larger decisions without it feeling scary.

Create healthy, winning decisions

I am not interested in where clients were or what they used to be like, or the mistakes they may have made. Sure, I will always listen to their recollections of painful childhoods or why certain things trigger those memories and affect them today, but I won't let them wallow in the past. They may as well drive while looking out of the rear window.

Feeling the fear and doing it anyway

My dear friend **Jon Fallows** inspires me as he has self-belief. Jon is employed by Sir Elton John as his personal hairstylist, and was previously stylist to Johnny Depp, Sienna Miller, Catherine Zeta-Jones and many other Hollywood stars, yet he is one of the most humble people I know.

Jon said:

I was inspired by Vidal Sassoon. I trained to be a hairdresser at the Vidal Sassoon Academy in Manchester. It was the best training I could have wished for. I am passionate about my work and I have a great rapport with my boss. This is the only job I have done where my boss allows me to be myself and supports and encourages me to grow as an individual. Rejection has never bothered me as I remain positive and trust that the universe is guiding me on the right path. Sometimes, however, I have wanted something so much that I have lost sight of whether or not it is right for me.

I have always had self-belief and 15 years ago I was a dancer on a commercial and the hairdresser's assistant didn't turn up, so I said: 'I can give you a hand if you like. I'm a hairdresser.' After much persuasion she agreed. Six months later that same hairdresser called asking if I wanted to work on a movie with her. I had no idea until I turned up at Pinewood Studios that it was *The Fifth Element* with Bruce Willis. My first day I thought 'Holy crap, what am I doing here?' I worked so hard and gave it 100% and have never looked back. I stayed working in film, TV and theatre and trained in wig-making and wig-dressing, and I know 100% now that this is the job I was put on this Earth to do. For most of my life I have wasted time with people who were horrible to me. At the age of 41 I thought life is too short to put up with selfish, unkind people and I made a healthy decision to do a slight culling of all the people who were energy vampires — it was challenging. As with any challenge I face, I have to teach myself that I can do it and not shy away. I feel so much more confident when I take responsibility for my life as my life is so much better, more productive, and I have more of a sense of calmness. I feel more positive in my outlook and keep remembering I can do it.

Jon's top tips. *If someone shows you who they really are, believe them. Consider others' feelings and remember that kindness, loyalty and sincerity will take you a long way. Always have self-belief: you can do it.*

Annie's thoughts. *By taking control of his life and practising self-belief, Jon feels more confident, calm and positive.*

Overcome adversity

Many argue that their problem or current situation is insoluble. This is not only a negative response but a clear sign to me that there is stinking thinking, fear and a lack of self-belief. Making decisions often means taking risks, which is a necessary part of self-development and plays a huge part in achieving success.

Sure, it's always good to learn from others when making decisions, but take my word here, it's never helpful to take advice from anyone unless they also share their strategy, techniques and tips for overcoming tragedy, financial hardship, pain and obstacles to achieve success, so you can learn from them. I would say 'Thanks but no thanks' to anyone offering advice – either solicited or unsolicited – who is coming from a position of cynicism, fear, jealousy and lack of self-belief.

Stay persistent

Persistence is a huge part of self-belief. It's a numbers game, and the majority of people will drop out so it's crucial that you keep going if you want to succeed in life. I assure you, eventually you will get to where you want to be.

Many people spend a crazy amount of time trying to hold on to what they have, what feels safe and familiar, and avoiding what they fear. Action is the key to overcoming fear. Why not be persistent with your new thoughts and actions, rather than persisting in not making changes?

'I tell my kids, if you lie down people will step all over you. If you keep scrambling, if you keep going, someone will always, always, give you a hand, always. But you gotta keep dancing, you gotta keep your feet moving.'
Morgan Freeman

If you don't confront your fears, they will run your entire life. Whenever you invest money and it goes wrong, why not look at it objectively and realise it's a sign to show you how to be wiser about investing next time? Why blame the company, the adviser, the friend who tipped you off, and decide never to invest again?

When you get hurt, do you take this as a lesson to trust your intuition next time or to take more time when choosing a partner or friend? Or do you moan about the situation and then believe you will get hurt again? Few people who are made redundant take it as a sign that perhaps the universe is guiding them to set up the business they always dreamed of or to go back to college, or as a suggestion to take time out and travel the globe. They often rush to find another job to get security as quickly as possible. So many people who lack self-belief are driven by fear, and they believe in other fearful people's opinions and stop following their dreams. It is so very sad!

John turns his life around:

I came to see Annie because my self-belief and self-confidence were at an all-time low. I had been made redundant and my partner left me. I felt frozen with fear and, if I am honest, I was angry with society. I had no idea what I wanted to do and was chasing after every job going. The first thing Annie suggested was to observe my thoughts and beliefs when I felt depressed, unhappy or discontented. Then to look at the people who made me feel good and supported me and those who made me feel fearful, miserable and inferior. What situations made me feel alive, excited, inspired, and what situations made me feel stifled, stuck, defiant. I made a list and it surprised me, but I started to have clarity about where I had blamed others and was deluded. I then listed six of my natural abilities and strengths and recalled what I loved doing when I was younger that felt effortless. Annie asked me what I would do if I knew I wouldn't fail and what would I do if money were no object, and suddenly it dawned on me that all I ever wanted to do was be creative. As a banker, I was in my head all the time and I realise now I had been so intent on pleasing my family that I didn't persist with my dreams. I took a 'sensible' job. I never used to be driven by material success, but I became that way and slowly but surely my soul was being crushed. I didn't like the person I was becoming. Annie challenged me to look at my redundancy as a 'universal boot kick'. I have let go of friends who wanted me to get hammered every week-end and sit in the pity pot and complain. Now, I feel re-energised. Annie has helped me change my perspective and I have enrolled at Chelsea College of Art. As I am writing, I can't believe it is me I am writing about. I feel totally in awe of myself for the first time ever. Annie made it clear she would guide me and facilitate the programme, but I had to apply the tools for the changes to take place. I am eternally grateful for Annie's unwavering support and guidance. She said she would believe in me, until I started to believe in me, and she did. Thank you, Annie, so much.

Jon's top tips. *Persevere and don't give up at the first rejection. Believe in yourself and your dreams and don't allow anyone to divert you from your chosen path.*

Annie's thoughts. *Jon gave up on everything before even giving it a go. He had no self-belief and therefore always took the easy option, and it wasn't until he was fired and forced into changes that he changed his perspective.*

Fears or beliefs?

You need to determine what is a fear and what is a core belief. If you think that you will look foolish asking someone out, if you feel people will think you are an idiot when you give your speech at your friend's birthday, or if you worry that your boss won't agree to a raise, this is a fear and not a belief. Fear of taking an exam or giving a public talk is an emotional reaction to your beliefs. These emotional reactions are not based on what others think of you; they are fears from believing something negative about yourself.

What others think of you can trigger your own negative beliefs about yourself. Your limiting beliefs crush your self-esteem and stand in the way of your happiness. The problem is that, when you have repeat-ed them so many times, you believe them wholeheartedly. When you have done such an amazing job of convincing yourself that these negative beliefs are true, it takes discipline and determination to reframe them. These beliefs are stored in the subconscious.

The power of the subconscious mind must never be underestimated. When I trained to become a master hypnotherapist, I learned to understand the difference between the conscious and the subconscious mind, so in the next section I'll briefly explain what this is so you can consider changing your perspective.

A brief explanation of the mind

The two levels of consciousness are:

1. the conscious mind
2. the subconscious mind.

The conscious mind

The conscious mind is responsible for logic and reason. Here we gather information from our five senses and control all our actions. Whatever you smell, see, hear, touch and taste is stored in your brain as memory. Your conscious mind makes all your decisions. It is finite: it does not want anything to change. That's why so many people live mediocre lives. They live in constant fear, allowing their conscious mind to stop them taking action. The conscious mind keeps you believing all the limiting beliefs, such as the following.

- 'I will fail.'
- 'I won't be a success.'
- 'I won't lose weight.'
- 'I am never going to be as smart as my sister.'
- 'I will never get a degree.'
- 'I will never get a raise.'

The conscious mind is like the captain giving the orders, but in truth the crew below the deck are in control as they are the subconscious, which carries out the orders.

The conscious mind (the captain) communicates with the outside world and appears to be in charge, but the subconscious mind (the crew) is in charge of the memories and past experiences that form beliefs, habits and behaviours through thoughts, emotions, and dreams.

The secret is to override the conscious mind; this can be achieved through self-hypnosis, hypnotherapy, meditation, creative visualisation and positive statements.

Hypnotherapy is a scientifically effective technique that helps to change behaviour and bust old habits.

The power of the subconscious mind

Your conscious mind can only process around seven thoughts at any given moment, and yet your subconscious mind is so powerful it can assimilate up to 400 trillion responses at the same time. Making lasting changes and reframing old habits into new habits can only be done effectively at a subconscious level.

A 2010 survey of psychotherapy literature by Alfred Barrios in *American Health* magazine revealed that:

- psychoanalysis has a 38% recovery rate after 600 sessions
- cognitive behavioural therapy has a 72% recovery rate after 22 sessions
- hypnotherapy has a 93% recovery rate after six sessions.

This demonstrates the power of the intuition over the intellect. Hypnotherapy overrides our intellect and ego and works with the subconscious, where your intuition resides. It is the most researched therapy, with over 12,000 studies to date, and is recognised by the British Medical Association, British Psychological Society and National Institute for Health and Clinical Excellence. As a master hypnotherapist, I am convinced that the reason I have such great success with clients is because:

- I use my intuition
- the process we go through helps clients develop their own intuition
- we work with the subconscious mind throughout the session.

Your breathing and heartbeats are controlled by your subconscious. Your emotions are also controlled by your subconscious, it is where your beliefs and memories are stored and also the source of your intuition. It is the job of the subconscious to locate and provide the data you feed it and send it back to the conscious mind. Bear in mind that the subconscious does not know the difference between what is real and what is false.

Visualise your success

One of the most powerful tools for changing limiting beliefs is visualisation. So many people tell me they believe that it works and yet they don't use it. If you are not willing to do whatever it takes and be disciplined, then you do not want to make the changes you say you do. Athletes are disciplined, and in all competitive sports visualisation techniques are considered the norm.

'I believe in creative visualisation.'

Victoria Beckham

Visualisation can change your life

Jo Fairley was a fan of creative visualisation way before it became known to the masses. Jo is co-founder of the organic chocolate empire Green & Blacks, having left school at 16 and becoming a secretary. Jo is contributing editor to *You* magazine and co-author of *The Beauty Bible*.

Jo told me:

I was lucky enough to have Anita Roddick as my mentor. She was dynamic, funny, didn't give a damn what people thought of her and tried to make a difference. I still miss her. The best piece of advice I have ever been given was actually a postcard bought in Brighton saying 'If you don't do it, you will never know what would have happened if you had done it.' When I was 15, my careers teacher said to me: 'Jo

Fairley, if you ever become so much as a 'Girl Friday' I will eat my hat. (I was a pretty nightmarish schoolgirl — slightly rebellious, argumentative and skated through my exams by the skin of my teeth.) I was absolutely determined from that moment on that I would do whatever I could to prove that I could be a success, which meant studying, working hard and grasping every opportunity that came my way. I am so grateful to her. When I was 14, I papered the inside of my wardrobe with photographs cut from magazines of places I wanted to go, people I wanted to know. I ended up going to those places and, extraordinarily enough, meeting many of those people, over the years. I now know it's called creative visualisation. I also wanted to 'make a difference' — I am a *Blue Peter* child and the idea of giving back and helping others less fortunate than myself was drummed into me at school, via TV and in my own family.

Jo's top tips. *Like my mentor Anita Roddick advised me, try not to care too much about what other people think, but stay true to your own belief about what needs to be done. Always surround yourself with positive people, not Eeyores.*

Annie's thoughts. *How amazing that Jo papered the inside of her wardrobe and made it into her vision board, creating opportunities that all came true.*

> 'I do believe, and I have seen it in my own life, that creative visualisation works.'
>
> Oprah

What is creative visualisation?

Creative visualisation is largely a right-brain function, and we can be trained by others or teach ourselves how to use it more effectively.

Research shows that visualisations during hypnotherapy enabled nationally-ranked Stanford male gymnasts to execute for the first time several complex routines in one session that they had been working on for over a year. They were able to eliminate timing errors, increase flexibility and possibly concentrate their strength.

If you talk to your brain it can get bored, but draw it a picture and it's way more interested, which is why it responds so well to visualisation.

Winning $112 million through visualisation

Cynthia Stafford was a single mother who was always interested in making the world a better place. She was working full time when one of her brothers died, leaving behind five children. Cynthia gave up her job, and after lengthy battles with the courts she was finally able to take custody of her brother's children. She wanted to give them and the rest of her family a better life and to contribute toward society in some way, so she decided to put to the test the visualisation technique she had read about in Dr Joseph Murphy's book *The Power of Your Subconscious Mind*.

She planned a strategy and she started the process. She was very focused on her dream, which was to become a philanthropist and to follow the principle she had always lived by: 'Give to others and it will come back to you.'

She designed the equivalent of a business plan and spent four months working on her plan to manifest $112 million.

After four months of visualising $112 million using Dr Murphy's techniques, she bought a lottery ticket for California's Mega Millions and won ... exactly $112 million.

Today, she has become a notable philanthropist and set up Cynthia Stafford's Foundation. Since winning the lottery in 2007, she has invested considerably in arts, women and children. She shared her winnings with her father and surviving brother and donated vast amounts to the Geffen Theatre and other non-profit organisations. She also hosts events regularly to raise awareness and education about domestic violence. Having given to charities all her life she continues to be an avid and active supporter of UNICEF. Cynthia swears the secret to winning that amount through the visualisation process was firstly empowering herself by using her brain to its fullest potential, and secondly taking control of her life by having a clear strategic plan for achieving what she wanted.

I use this example as
- it illustrates the power of the mind
- it illustrates the importance of focus
- it illustrates that when you are clear about what you want and you use the visualisation technique, you have the power to bring amazing results into your life.

You can plan a strategy to win a race, travel the world, run a successful business or build a dream home, and use the visualisation process to help you manifest it.

Annie's thoughts. *As this experience demonstrates, creative visualisation is incredibly powerful. However, the brain doesn't know the difference between fantasy and reality so be careful what you wish for.*

Reasons to believe it

In case you may be sceptical about this, let me share a little of the brain research that has discovered the science behind the effects of visualisation. If you visualise lifting your right foot, it stimulates the same part of the brain that is activated when you actually lift your right foot. This shared area of brain activation where you imagine an action and perform it has been demonstrated extensively in scientific research.

In sports and athletics, visualisation is considered an integral aspect of training. Research reveals that part of the brain is responsible for creating a navigation plan for action. This part is called the posterior parietal cortex, and it processes information from the skin, the internal organs and the vision, and creates an internal model of the movement to be formed before it is actually carried out.

Dr Srini Pillay is a psychiatrist, brain researcher and coach. He emphasises the importance of visualising in the first person, to stimulate the neural pathways. Dr Pillay says: 'The posterior parietal cortex can become too overloaded with information while visualising, so it's important to break things down in stages so that your brain digests the information.' (*The New York Times*, November 2011.)

The steps of creative visualisation

1. Set a goal.
2. Be clear.
3. Be vivid.
4. Buy lots of magazines.
5. Buy a large piece of card (from an art shop).

Getting prepared

It's essential that you convey your objectives to your subconscious mind. Be very goal-oriented. If your goal is money, decide on the exact amount; if it is a partner, be clear about your timeline for meeting them; if it is a property, figure out when you want to move in; if it is a new job, be sure you know when you want to be starting there. Make your objective as vivid as watching a movie.

Create clear images, put yourself in the image, and, if it involves a partner, see yourself walking together. If you want a new car, see yourself driving it; if it's a new house, see yourself cooking in the kitchen. Enlarge it, light it up, and get creative.

Make the image bright, bold and large. Make it as real as possible. Don't forget: our subconscious cannot tell the difference between an image we are creating and the real thing.

Ready, steady, go

Keep your hands loose and don't cross your legs. Close your eyes and breathe normally. Focus on your breath to help banish negative thoughts from your busy mind. Your aim here is to bring in a purposeful, positive thought and focus all your energy on it so you can manifest it into your life. If you feel that you are relaxed and ready, start creating the desired images with you in them. Step into the image, feel it, sense it, embrace it, be it, live it, dream it, desire it, taste it, smell it and smile. Use all your emotions, and imagine it is happening right now. Feel the excitement of it being true for you right here, right now. Enlarge it. Make the image bold, bright and big; make it glaring. Then repeat 'Thank you, thank you, thank you', as if you have already received what you are imagining. I like to then put a gold outline and a huge white circle around the image and release it. I let it go when I have finished, so that I am letting go of how or when it will arrive. At the same time, I trust that it *will* arrive.

Think of it as like being in a restaurant. You give your order to the waiter, sit back and trust that what you've ordered will arrive. You do not insist on knowing exactly what time it will be delivered to your table or which door it will come out of. You don't go into the kitchen and watch the chef prepare it. You have ordered it, described it, asked for it, and you wait, trusting it will appear. I don't have a clue about how electricity works, but I know when I turn the switch the light comes on. I don't know how breathing works, but when I wake I am breathing and continue to do so all through the day. Analysing can be paralysing; give up a few minutes each day and visualise.

Vision board

Spend some time tearing out images and words from magazines and stick them onto your board. Get really creative. You may want one board for your personal life and one for your professional life.

Imagine the possibilities . . .
- These boards need to be placed somewhere you can see them regularly and are able to keep staring at them. If you live with flatmates and this isn't something you feel comfortable doing, cut the images out and stick them into a journal, diary or notepad and keep this with you at all times so you can flick

through and focus on the images and words for several minutes, several times a day.

- Take a photo with your phone of your vision board and put it on your desktop.
- If you have a phone that has a recorder on it, why not record positive statements and play them while visualising? Your subconscious mind will absorb the images and record them as real and valid. This is why it is essential to be clear and precise.

SUMMARY. THE ELIXIR OF SELF-BELIEF

- ◆ Every time you convince yourself you can't do something, your wish will be granted and you won't be able to do it.
- ◆ The only way to get rid of your old self-beliefs is to take action and walk through your fears. Show yourself you can do absolutely anything if you want to, and in turn this will send your confidence through the roof. You need to develop blind faith.
- ◆ You see only what you want to see, so stop believing in the lies. Your anxiety will go and so much will be easier in your life because you will have acquired faith in yourself.
- ◆ Rely on yourself, stand by yourself, and do not allow obstacles to prevent you from achieving what you want in life. It's always about perception, not reality.
- ◆ Gain clarity, learn about the subconscious and conscious minds, and start visualising.
- ◆ Honour yourself by never giving up on your dreams.

A call to action

1. The lessons I have learned about self-belief are:

....

....

2. A person or situation I have needed self-belief around is:

....

....

3. I would like to have self-belief because:

....

....

4. The excuses I might make to avoid the need for self-belief are:

....

....

5. The steps I will take to find self-belief are:

....

....

ANNIE'S CONFIDENCE-BOOSTERS FOR SELF-BELIEF

◆ Change your perceptions.
◆ Be clear about your individuality and preferences.
◆ Do not be discouraged by mistakes.
◆ Let go of self-defeating beliefs about what might happen in the future.
◆ Say over and over again 'I am good enough'.

Secret no. 6

SELF-RESPONSIBILITY

Successful people take responsibility for their own lives and have a commanding presence

'We are each responsible for our own life. No-one else is or can be.'

Oprah

Are you emotionally sober?

Being emotionally sober is being responsible for every area of your life. Self-responsibility is the foundation of empowerment. You are responsible for how you feel, what you think, the choices you make, the friends you choose to spend time with, the steps you take, your inaction or action, the way you respond to situations or people, the pain you feel and the happiness you create. You determine how your self-esteem and self-confidence develop. You are responsible for your health, energy and well-being, the time you spend on activities, the time you spend listening to others' issues, the time you invest in other people's lives. You are totally responsible for the behaviour you demonstrate: successful people demonstrate solution-focused behaviour and are assertive without being aggressive.

You are responsible for confronting your fears or running away from them, becoming stressed, becoming anxious, being fit, being overweight, getting enough sleep, the way you speak, your body language, your rigid or flexible views, and your opinions.

Jonathan Ross, on Channel 4's *Hotel GB*, was asked by Gordon Ramsay to offer advice to the unemployed trainees. He said: 'It's important you always take responsibility for yourself. Don't blame anyone else for your mistakes: own up, learn from them and move on.'

Implementing responsibility in your life

Shu Richmond is an award-winning producer, who has worked for many years on entertainment, factual, daytime and lifestyle television programmes, the most famous being ITV's *This Morning*. I asked Shu to give me her opinion of self-responsibility.

Shu told me:

My godmother, the TV presenter Judith Chalmers, inspired me. I am motivated by ideas and communicating them to others — a TV programme, a book, a product — creativity makes the world go round. It may sound a cliché, but the best advice I was given was 'be true to yourself'. Honesty and integrity are hugely important to me. Many problems, and especially in TV, arise from people trying to hide the truth or passing the blame on to someone else. Bosses or managers must not create a climate of fear — this leads to a damaging culture of blame. I admire those who are honest, witty, work hard and who have integrity and a generosity of spirit. I don't manage rejection well, but it's part of working in TV, as a huge amount of ideas are generated and few commissioned. Sure, listen to others and accept flaws if they exist in your idea, but have confidence in a good idea. Flaws can be fixed; an idea can be reworked to suit a particular channel. Responding to the first rejection by abandoning a good idea is a weakness. Many great projects, such as *Desperate Housewives*, *Who Wants To Be a Millionaire*, and *Slumdog Millionaire*, were turned down several times before being commissioned. Take responsibility for your idea by being open to feedback, learning from failures and rejection, and not allowing them to put you off developing your idea and submitting it again. You have to take responsibility for getting organised and creating a work—life balance. I advise everyone to follow their dream, but don't wait until you reach it to be happy. Happiness needs to be now. The journey is the best bit, so don't waste it worrying about what time you will arrive or what you will find.

Shu's top tips. *Take responsibility when things go wrong by owning up. Take responsibility for not giving up on your dreams.*

Annie's thoughts. *Shu demonstrates very clearly that it is down to each one of us to be self-responsible for our life, our actions, and our dreams.*

By not being accountable for your life, you give your power away and become dependent on others' approval. You don't take risks, and you may become addicted to unhealthy habits – drinking too much, eating too much, smoking, gambling, random sex . . .

- 'I never have luck.'
- 'Life is unfair.'
- 'It's my parents' fault.'
- 'I am the way I am.'
- 'I cannot handle this.'
- 'He/she made me feel that way.'
- 'I didn't want to but he/she made me.'

Reprogramme your thoughts

Many who lack confidence quit, stay stuck, become aggressive, have blind spots, minimise or deny the truth, constantly make excuses as to why they can't change or move forward, blame society, schooling, family, lack of money, the government, the economy … They constantly complain, are full of repressed anger, are in denial, are often co-dependent, are pessimistic, are negative or are martyrs.

Successful people have self-confidence and are emotionally sober, which means that they are in control of their life. They are proactive and would never be caught moaning, groaning or blaming. They are aware that everything has a consequence – either negative or positive, depending on their choice and their action – and they own their part in everything. They do not view being accountable as a burden, but instead as the door to freedom. They focus on what they want in life, not what they don't want. They take 100% responsibility for their life and create opportunities and positive results. They have often gone through terrible things but they don't allow this to hold them back.

'The person who says it cannot be done must not interrupt the person who wants to do it.'

Chinese proverb

Successful people don't complain about the way their parents were or stay stuck on what happened to them as a youngster. Many find it in their heart to forgive, and those who cannot still do not use that as an excuse to relinquish responsibility.

By dwelling on your own unworthiness, lack of confidence and low self-esteem, you find any excuse to keep your life small. When you are jealous of others who achieve success it's because you are not maximising your own potential. Self-confidence, self-motivation and self-responsibility are the cornerstones to success.

Unstoppable you

Successful people are motivated and this is why they get results. They do not wait for others to motivate them; they motivate themselves. They have the willingness to be responsible and are eager, passionate, enthusiastic and ambitious enough to want to change their life. Their confidence and belief in themselves, coupled with passion, are what drive them forward and motivate them.

Action is essential to achieving success and excelling in life. Those who lack motivation lack confidence, focus, direction and self-belief. Many say: 'Why bother? Because I won't succeed.' You will never be motivated if you are unwilling to give something a go, so you must take responsibility for yourself. Can you see that?

> 'My motivations have changed a lot over the past 40 years. In retrospect, it is clear this has been a long-term process, and I acquire new motivations over time. . . . I am constantly challenging my team with new ideas, innovations or ventures I would like to set up . . . You may wonder if such adventures are appropriate for a man my age — 60 — which brings me to my last motivational rule: "Screw it, let's do it." '
> Richard Branson, www.entrepreneur.com, 4 May 2011

A commanding presence

Successful people are aware how essential effective communication skills are and how important first impressions are. Successful people take full responsibility for their choices, actions, words, thoughts and feelings and create their own opportunities. They know that self-responsibility and respect go hand in hand. It's interesting that those who duck out of responsibility blame others for what has gone wrong, but I notice they don't ever credit others with their success.

There is a TV series based in an airport where passengers blame absolutely everything and everybody else for missing their flight. They rant, they rave, they get nasty or sarcastic, their ego inflates, but not once have I ever heard anyone admit they ought to have had an earlier night so they wouldn't have missed their train, taxi or lift. Not once have I heard anyone admit that they ought to have checked their passport hadn't expired or checked the time on their ticket or read the small print or left the bar in the terminal earlier so they would have heard the announcements heard by everyone else who was boarding.

'The price of greatness is responsibility.'
Sir Winston Churchill

Most problems at work can be traced back to something interpersonal. Successful people stay committed to and passionate about their decisions, but are flexible in their approach. They are aware that if they blame someone else, they give away their power to change.

Successful people step forward boldly and embrace responsibility, whereas most people do absolutely everything in life to avoid it. Those who are successful also mess up, but they 'fess up.

'Life is a gift, and it offers us the privilege, opportunity and responsibility to give something back by becoming more.'
Anthony Robbins

Everything is a choice

Many deflect and create distractions by watching excess television, surfing the net, lazing around or gossiping. All of this stagnates our growth. Many people become so mired in these distractions that they then blame others when things don't work out the way they want or move forward with something. This is immature behaviour, not emotionally sober behaviour. Another way to shirk our responsibility to ourselves is to spend hours investing time and energy in other people's issues, rather than looking at what we need to be getting on with. In fact, this is a form of self-neglect.

'The world needs dreamers, the world needs doers, but most of all the world needs dreamers who are doers.'

Richard Reed, co-founder of Innocent Drinks, on BBC's Be Your Own Boss, September 2012

The kindest thing you can do for yourself is take responsibility for what you think, need, want and feel. I am not saying you must not take care of others or help others, but I am saying you need to find the balance, and, most importantly, be accountable to yourself before identifying your responsibilities to others. You must have enough self-respect to take care of yourself. Own your part in things: it is essential you do not allow yourself to be swayed by anyone who is manipulative or playing games. When others talk nonsense or act irresponsibly, let them. You don't have to follow them and play along; you can own your own power, act in a mature way, trust your instincts and not discount yourself. Take a risk and go with what feels right for you, as you can't wait around for a guarantee in life – you may end up waiting *all* your life. If it all goes wrong, you can learn from it. Ignore anyone who says 'I told you so' and remain responsible for your choices, as this is what will strengthen your courage muscles.

Having a winner's attitude

I spoke to **Arabella Dymoke**, food editor on *The Good Web Guide*, who took responsibility for her dreams. She wanted to own the business, and so in 2008 she bought out her partners. Today Amazon describes the guide as 'The Orient Express of web navigation', and in less than four years it has become a firmly recognised brand name, supported by many high-profile entrepreneurs.

Arabella told me:

I was inspired by Natalie Massenet (Net-a-Porter.com) and Martha Lane Fox (lastminute.com), who were trailblazing at the beginning of the dotcom boom and continue to do so today. Natalie is not only an icon of fashion, but an icon of the web. I have suffered a lot of rejection but I don't let it affect me; I just get back up and on the case. With any challenges I face, I break each one down into hurdles and that way they seem more surmountable. It's crucial to be tenacious, take responsibility for yourself and never accept no for an answer. My motivation comes from passion for my business and the pace of the internet and innovation. I find others who give generously and share their time and expertise a real inspiration.

Arabella's top tips. *If you are in doubt about something, act on it straight away as the longer you delay making a decision about changing something the more fear creeps in and the longer it takes to recover your position.*

Annie's thoughts. *It's impressive that Arabella was working for a company and, instead of resenting the fact that it wasn't hers, she took control of her life and bought the business. Also, rather than being jealous of Natalie and Martha for their success, she salutes them. That's emotional sobriety.*

Experiment; try something new; *just do it.* Don't wait for approval or permission from anyone else — it is *your* life. Successful people know what is best for them and what is right for them. They know the only opinion they require is their own. They know that fear and anxiety block solutions; ships only sail well in calm seas, so they stay calm.

> 'It is time to restore the American precept that each individual is accountable for his or her actions.'
>
> Ronald Reagan

When you lack confidence you do not recognise your own self-worth. The paradox here is that you become almost disposable to yourself and your life becomes focused on others' wants and needs. It's very nice to help others, but so many people feel that others deserve their help yet they themselves don't. Going to the other extreme, are you being self-centred, not helping anyone at all but rather relinquishing all self-responsibility and looking for others to do everything for you? Neither of these approaches will build your confidence, so you need to be somewhere in the middle.

The power of questions

Successful people know that to have a powerful exchange with someone, they must ask effective questions. This also helps reduce misunderstandings. How do you feel when you're out with someone or networking with them and they do not ask a single question?

If you aren't inquisitive, you are assuming you know all there is to know. By asking powerful questions you encourage reflective, thought-provoking conversations. It's essential that you don't assume, because that can ruin the flow of the conversation; in fact, it's arrogant to do so. Ask in a gentle but assertive way whatever you want to know, because this will stimulate reflective conversations.

Use the following powerful questions.

- 'What if xyz?'
- 'How about xyz?'
- 'Why is that important to you?'
- 'Where does that take place?'
- 'When will that be happening?'

Successful people sharpen their powers of observation and train themselves to listen, suspending all assumptions,, They know that assumptions can lead to damaged relationships, unfulfilled responsibilities, stress and all sorts of negative consequences, both personally and professionally.

Successful people take their time to ask thoughtful questions. Those lacking in confidence ramble, tune out or offer ideas, opinions and unsolicited feedback. Most people who lack confidence wouldn't think to stop for a moment to ask for someone else's thoughts or to inquire what someone else's perspective is. Others may do this, but for approval rather than from a sincere interest in getting to know the other person.

> *'People are multifaceted. We must let others function in a way that allows them to shine.'*
>
> Donald Trump

Practise 'being' rather than 'doing'

Lacking in confidence means fidgeting, playing with a pen or your hair, tapping fingers on a table, talking fast, looking around the room to see who else is there, interrupting a speaker and looking down. If you do any of these things, it advertises your insecurity and lack of confidence.

Confident, successful people calm angry people down, energise lethargic people, and ask for clarification when they don't understand something. They create synergy and understanding, they use non-judgemental language, and they come up with strategies for solving problems. They focus on actions, not attitudes, and when they have a difficult situation to discuss, they dismiss all emotional charge and stick to the facts, speaking with the voice of sanity and reason.

How to create an impact

Confident people know when to start a conversation, when to end it, and how to build a rapport. To acquire these new skills I recommend checking out YouTube: study the body language of Tony Robbins when he gives a motivational talk; observe Steve Jobs mastering his presentations; watch Karren Brady deliver her opinions on *The Apprentice*; watch President Obama deliver his speeches; watch how Madonna pauses before answering a question during an interview. Look at her posture. Become a master of your body and mind and take responsibility for your appearance, your actions, your words and your energy. Pay particular attention when studying masters of verbal and non-verbal communication. In the 'Further reading' chapter, I have suggested some excellent books you can refer to.

Remember: when you are meeting someone, whether it be for work or personally, you are generally 'selling' yourself on some level. You are sussing out whether the other person (or people) are buying into what you are offering. You are looking for an interaction that keeps them interested.

Successful people know that it's not all about them. They listen, empathise, question and engage, showing interest in the other person. They don't stand there and take the other person hostage by speaking non-stop about themselves. This is unattractive and arrogant and comes from the ego, self-centredness and a lack of awareness and sensitivity.

Stand up, own who you are and honour yourself

'If someone has something to say I prefer they say it to my face.'

Simon Cowell

I was at a networking event and having a conversation when someone sidled up and interrupted us. She proceeded to speak about herself and her upcoming event. I said: 'You have charged up to us and butted into our conversation, which I find totally unacceptable, and then you have taken me hostage by speaking about yourself and your event, without even having the courtesy to ask my name or ask about me. I find your behaviour unreasonable.'

She looked shocked and walked away, and my colleague looked shocked too. Why do I need to tolerate such bad behaviour? Why did my colleague feel that it was acceptable? Why didn't the woman I confronted have any awareness or sensitivity about her behaviour, or take responsibility for her actions?

My colleagues said: 'At last someone said something. She comes monthly and does that all the time, but no-one wants to upset her.'

So, should everyone allow rude people to continue being rude and not say anything? They can offend a room full of people, but you must not offend them? I find that very odd. How dishonest would it have been of me if I had smiled and said nothing? I would have been demonstrating that her time, energy and words were important and mine were not.

I was not aggressive, nor insulting. I was honest and assertive. I have the confidence to say what I mean and mean what I say. I do not need her approval or anyone else's.

Direct, open and honest

Many years ago I was at a book launch for an old friend, the highly successful Ian Marber, aka the Food Doctor. I left before the end as I had a commitment. Ian called me the next day and asked why I had left without saying goodbye. I replied: 'I thought it would be rude to interrupt you while you were having a conversation.' His reply cracked me up: 'Yes, absolutely right, it would have been.' I love that Ian always says it as it is.

Being upfront

When someone says it as it is, it's highly unlikely they will be gossiping about you behind your back; they will have already said what they wanted to say to your face. You always know where you stand with direct people – you know how they feel and what they think. It is so refreshing to be around assertive, direct people. You don't have to tiptoe around and be fake. Successful people are accountable for what they feel and think. They are not victims, they are emotionally sober and they are sensitive to our feelings. They are not aggressive, but neither do they need you to approve of them. They know who they are and what they want and where they are going.

> Just that little bit of skill and confidence changes everything. I had to stop going to auditions thinking "I hope they like me". I had to go in thinking I was

the answer to all their problems. You could feel the difference in the room immediately. The greatest lesson I learned was that you have to be willing to fail.'

George Clooney

Be honest, do you:

- ☐ jump in when others are talking?
- ☐ talk over others?
- ☐ not really listen to what other people are saying?
- ☐ look around the room to see who else is there?
- ☐ allow others to take you hostage?
- ☐ talk about yourself and not ask questions?
- ☐ react quickly with a defensive tone if criticised?
- ☐ strive to be a peace-maker and avoid conflict?
- ☐ often say yes when you mean no?
- ☐ communicate in a bold way?
- ☐ make out that everything is fine when it isn't, and change the subject?
- ☐ feel motivated by the need to know, analyse and understand everything?
- ☐ express thoughts rather than feelings?
- ☐ build on others' ideas rather than criticise?
- ☐ inspire confidence and trust in others?
- ☐ often ask 'what if'?
- ☐ communicate by sharing personal stories about yourself?

Some people do not find it easy to say what they feel in a personal situation. Do not attack them for this. Be compassionate and rational and understand that's the way it is with them. Work out what your needs are and what is acceptable to you and what is not. Sit down with them and share it.

'I enjoy real people, down-to-earth people who are true to themselves and honest to your face — good or bad.'

Christina Aguilera

Successful people don't use sarcasm. That's passive-aggressive and this book is not about teaching anyone to be aggressive, nor about supporting anyone in being passive – it is about being confident, and confident people do not rely on sarcasm. It is the same as manipulation, and a cowardly way of saying something you don't have the confidence to say directly.

Having a lack of confidence also means you are so busy being right and forcing your opinions on others when you communicate that you dominate the conversation, and are usually pretty tactless with your remarks. You are not really bothered about anyone else so you rattle on, completely self-absorbed. Often, when you lack confidence you try to convince others, when in fact you are really trying to convince yourself. Successful people are excellent communicators. They are comfortable with themselves so they don't try to impress others; it's all about delivering clear, concise information in a succinct way and genuinely listening to the speaker and their point of view without being judgemental.

'Think beyond the traditional boundaries. Learn the value of saying no. View a conflict as an opportunity.'

Donald Trump

What is your style?

Are you a tough communicator?

- You are driven, energetic and committed.
- You are assertive.
- Your main concern is to win by doing it your way.

Are you a friendly communicator?

- You are flexible, gentle and open-minded.
- You are co-operative, easy-going and trusting.
- You are concerned with having 'positive relationships'.

Are you a logical communicator?

- You are calm, pragmatic and organised.
- You use facts, detail and common sense.
- Your priorities are knowledge and information.

Does your style currently work for you?

Years ago, I was dating someone who constantly talked about himself and never once asked a question about me. He told me all about his ex-wife and his business and his visions, and after a few dates I decided to call it a day as I felt I could have been a cardboard cut-out and he wouldn't have noticed. Call me old-fashioned, but I feel the purpose of dates is to get to know each other, so surely that involves a two-way conversation?

LISTENING EXERCISE

1. Find a friend and then choose a subject you disagree on – clothes, politics, books, values, potential partners. Set your alarm for three minutes. One of you talks about the chosen topic and then you swap over. How was it? Did either of you interrupt the other? Did both of you listen? Did you both have direct eye contact and stay still and focused during the three minutes?

2. Choose a colleague. Ask them to describe in detail how they get to work. Then repeat it back to them word by word. How was it? Was it a challenge to hear and stay focused? Did either of you speak over the other?

Our communication skills are learned behaviours; but remember: sometimes change can happen quickly, sometimes slowly. The secret of improving your communication skills is practice, practice, practice.

Successful people have the skill of being able to make everyone they speak to feel as if they are the only person who exists. Successful people are not wrapped up in their own story. They are not distracted, self-conscious, irritable, vague, uncomfortable, rambling, speaking too fast, behaving in a disingenuous manner or feeling awkward. They are aware of how the other person is responding to them. They spontaneously add to the conversation and understand that rapport is the most important and fundamental ingredient – without it we are unlikely to get very far.

Learn to listen and listen to learn

When listening, always listen out for the similarities, not the differences. This is important when in a challenging situation with a colleague or a loved one. So many people polarise the issues and demonise the other person. They do this because they don't have self-confidence and need to puff themselves up to feel superior and 'better' than the other person; they constantly listen out for differences so they can flag up others' shortcomings and make themselves feel better.

Everyone wants to be around someone who is positive, warm and caring, and asks questions then genuinely listens to their answers. Successful people interact, they share interesting topics, exchange information, pool their experiences, are respectful of others' opinions, even if they don't agree, and when they talk it flows as they are acting in a congruent way, with passion and sincerity. They know that listening and hearing are not the same thing, and that building a rapport is crucial professionally and personally. They know it's perfectly acceptable to stand up and speak up, to mean what they say and say what they mean. They know how to say no with ease and confidence. They know their opinions and views are important and worth considering. They master the art of effective communication and learn the best strategies for dealing with difficult people and difficult situations. They look the part; they sound the part; they behave the part. They have a commanding presence because they stand still and listen to someone else, looking them directly in the eye, showing that they are interested and asking effective questions.

Focus on:

- breathing
- facial expressions
- voice tone, pitch and speed
- active listening.

Why do we need to listen?

- to learn
- to understand
- to enjoy
- to obtain information.

Determined, dedicated and principled

I asked my dear friend **Ted Johnson**, deputy editor of *Variety* magazine, about the importance of listening skills. *Variety* was founded in 1905 in New York before moving to LA and is Hollywood's premier weekly guide, on sale in 60 countries. It presents the 'must know' news of the showbiz industry, exclusive reports and behind-the-scenes coverage.

Ted told me:

My parents inspired me. I am the youngest of 10 children and they gave us a pretty idyllic middle-class childhood, and they now say they don't remember worrying much about anything, which I find so inspirational. The most successful friends I have are the ones who want to help you; it's such a gift to know them. My mother used to tell me all the time when I was in high school that when I get agitated, anxiety-ridden or doubtful, to just pause. That's saved me from saying something I will regret or, most importantly, sending an email. As I got older, I started to look at rejection as something that is not meant to be for now, which is perhaps a more spiritual way of looking at it. But as a writer and an editor, I realise that there are so many variables, like timing, that go into journalism. It's not as fateful as say, acting, but professional relationships do matter in this career.

My biggest challenge was coming out at 31. I did a whole range of things to get through the fear — I read books (*The Best Little Boy in the World* by Andrew Tobias), went to 'coming out' meetings at the Gay and Lesbian Centre in Los Angeles, talked to my church pastor, got counselling, but the best advice came from a friend who said: 'If you come out and I am the only one who accepts you, will you be OK?' I said 'Yes,' and of course it turned out to be nothing but positive. Going through it at the time, you think it is the big elephant in the room, and always will be. Many years later, it's amazing how ho-hum it all seems. Regards listening skills — Stewart, my husband, will probably laugh at this as he is always trying to get my attention, over my phone and my computer, but I do truly believe my listening skills are important to my success. They are essential in life and more so for me as I interview people, go to speeches, witness events and then write about them.

Ted's top tips. *Don't be afraid to take risks and make mistakes. Also, never underestimate how crucial it is to possess listening skills.*

Annie's thoughts. *Ted is not only an inspiration for having the courage to come out as he did at 31, but he has also grown up being taught the power of pausing and having sound emotional control, so he can respond rather than react when agitated. A great skill to have.*

Staying focused

Listening and hearing are two different things. Listening requires focus and means paying attention to the verbal and non-verbal messages from the speaker. Many people are so self-centred that they only half-listen to others while focusing on their shopping, emails or catching the train, and thinking they are maybe missing out on something else. How amazing does it feel when someone genuinely listens to you, and how offensive is it when they are clearly not listening?

If you are shuffling papers, picking your nails, fidgeting your feet from impatience and looking out of the window because you are oh-so important and you just don't have the time to listen, why on earth would you expect anyone to listen to you?

A good listener will let go of all preconceived ideas and be open and flexible. They will try to understand things from someone else's point of view. They never finish a sentence for someone else and they never leap in the moment the speaker has paused. They will watch facial expressions and eye movements, absorb and process them, and then reflect back to the speaker to ensure they have understood fully.

'If we were supposed to talk more than listen, we would have two tongues and one ear.'

Mark Twain

Transforming relationships

Successful people do not have expectations and prejudices that can lead to false assumptions, and therefore they don't jump to incorrect conclusions. I cannot stress how powerful it is to have effective listening skills and how much this helps us have a commanding presence.

When someone speaks, it's important you ask yourself whether you are listening to the words of the speaker and you understand what they are saying. Are you relating to what they are saying? Many feel they are listening when they are in a dialogue and not speaking.

However, that's not always listening, although it may appear to be if you haven't learned listening skills yourself.

Effective listening skills can transform relationships both in and outside work. Our average attention span is around 22 seconds. Most people think that to get their point across they have to raise their voice, shout or interrupt the other person. It's like the Englishman abroad: when speakers of another language don't respond to his request in English, he speaks louder. However, they aren't deaf; it's just that they don't speak English. It's like some of the adverts on TV that shout at us. Do they think no-one can hear? It's bizarre . . .

Are you aware that effective listening is a choice? Are you aware that you can change the way you respond, communicate and listen? Are you aware that sometimes you may choose not to listen to someone who is saying something you are avoiding or refuse to accept?

Reflective listening

This is when you listen to yourself, your inner voice. You pause before you respond to a question, a situation or a remark. You allow your intuition to guide you about what to say and how best to respond. It's very powerful; rather than go with an instant response to what you are asked, if you pause for around 20 seconds you can often give a much more profound answer. This is because:

- you are listening to the other person with complete focus
- you are listening to yourself.

Often our minds wander when others are talking, so practise undivided attention and train yourself to be in the present moment. It will transform your communication skills radically and hugely improve your listening skills, and help you have a commanding presence.

This is a powerful exercise to use in a professional capacity – the more you discipline yourself to pause before answering, the more you will be guided as to the best questions to ask, and this can bring about much more effective results. Also, if you are communicating with a tricky colleague, client or boss, pausing will help you become more conscious and allow you to step back from the situation. It will help you to come from a more grounded and connected place if you use those 20 seconds to say to yourself: 'That's the way Sue is. She is not who I feel or think she should be, she is who she is, and if I want to make this work then I need to accept that and listen to her from a different perspective and try to understand her point of view and where she is coming from, rather than making this all about me.'

This doesn't work if someone is being abusive, but in all other cases you can use reflective listening to change the way you view your relationship and change the outcome of the situation.

Active listening

This is when you demonstrate that you are actively listening to the speaker. I have been in situations where I can see that someone has tuned out; I immediately stop talking as I refuse to waste my precious energy speaking when I'm not being heard. I have been at many dinner parties where someone is going on and on and it is pretty obvious no-one is interested, but they haven't come up for air because they have zero self-awareness and sensitivity to others. Also, the way you listen to others often has an impact on the way they listen to you in return. Others will be much more receptive when you offer them presence, silence, and reflective and active listening skills.

I once had a date with someone who asked: 'Do you like James Brown?' I said: 'He was amazingly talented, but not really my scene.'

He said: 'Do you know the track xyz?' I said: 'Like I say, he is not really my scene.'

He then spent 10 minutes with me as a captive audience (we were sitting in traffic) going on and on about this track. I have nothing against James Brown, but as I said, he is not my scene. I was on a date, but firstly my date wasn't listening, and secondly he showed no sensitivity towards me as I couldn't have made it more obvious that I had no interest. Needless to say, that was my last date with him, as these small yet crucial clues reveal someone's character.

Imagine something similar happens at an interview, and you do not listen actively to what the interviewer is saying. It could seriously mess up your chances of getting the job.

> 'Knowledge speaks but wisdom listens.'
>
> Jimi Hendrix

I also had a phone call from a personal development organisation that wanted me to attend a course. For various reasons, I do not hold this organisation in high regard, so I thanked the woman for calling but said I wasn't interested. She talked over me about all the benefits and what I would be passing up, so I said: 'Are you a qualified coach?'

'Yes,' she replied. I said: 'When I was trained, they drummed into us the importance of listening skills. You are so busy wanting to have your needs met by selling me a course, you have no interest in asking what my needs are or hearing me when I say no.'

She didn't apologise or even seem to understand what on earth I was saying, which is pretty worrying when you consider that she was representing an organisation in the personal development world. By actively listening you are acknowledging the speaker by nodding your head or saying 'uh-huh'; this also helps you stay focused on what the speaker is saying. If you are looking for information, it also encourages the speaker to continue speaking. I cannot emphasise enough how loudly non-verbal language speaks. Smile and nod from time to time. As a listener, your role is to understand what is being said. By actively listening you can say 'What I am hearing is ...' or 'Am I correct in understanding that you meant...?'

Summarise, paraphrase and give feedback

Make sure you summarise the speaker's comments periodically. However, always ensure that you allow the speaker to finish their sentence or their point before you ask a question. When you do ask questions, do so assertively and respectfully. Concentrate fully on what the speaker's message is and reflect and actively demonstrate that you are listening by paraphrasing that message. So often what someone says to us and what we hear are completely different. Any of you who watch *The Apprentice* will know that this has caused candidates to lose tasks many times, because they didn't listen to what was being asked of them. Your productivity at work will improve profoundly and your personal and professional relationships will also change for the better if you improve your listening skills.

Successful people know that when they speak their truth, it can often give others the confidence to speak theirs. They also know when to hold back and listen to the other person's point of view without judgement or defensiveness – especially when the other person has a different view to theirs – rather than giving unsolicited advice, correcting them or offering answers.

Example of respectful feedback could be:

- 'That's an interesting way to view it.'
- 'I will take on board what you said.'
- 'This is obviously something you feel passionate about.'

This type of feedback can be very effective in personal situations, but equally effective professionally if a colleague is angry or upset, because it means acknowledging what they are saying but not having to agree with or criticise them.

Successful people do not half-listen while planning their defence. They make a conscious effort to allow people to finish what they are saying. However, if someone interrupts them while they are speaking, they hold their own with remarks such as:

- 'I have not finished speaking. Please hold on to your thoughts until I have finished.'
- 'I would like to add to this conversation and am finding it difficult to do so. Could you please wait until I have finished?'
- 'I would appreciate it if you would let me finish before leaping in.'

SUMMARY. INTEGRATING SELF-RESPONSIBILITY INTO YOUR LIFE

◆ If you evade responsibility you allow others to control, manipulate or interrupt you, score points, apply pressure, put you down, make assumptions and dictate what you ought to do.

◆ When taking responsibility you design your life, champion yourself, have focus, clarity and integrity, and use concise, coherent and concrete communication.

◆ Learn to listen and listen to learn. Polish your communication skills and respect others as you want to be respected. Create an impact.

◆ You must realise that you are important, unique and worthy.

A call to action

1. The lessons I have learned about self-responsibility are:

....

....

2. A person or situation I have needed self-responsibility around is:

....

....

3. I would like to start being responsible for myself because:

....

....

4. The excuses I might make to avoid taking self-responsibility are:

....

....

5. The steps I will take to start being responsible for myself are:

....

....

ANNIE'S CONFIDENCE-BOOSTERS FOR SELF-RESPONSIBILITY

- ◆ Caring for others works; caretaking them doesn't.
- ◆ You need to set limits with others.
- ◆ Self-care is not selfish, it is self-loving.
- ◆ Don't wait to be rescued – take action.
- ◆ Say over and over again 'I have a responsibility to be good to myself.'

Secret no. 7

SELF-ASSERTIVENESS

Successful people are proactive,
bold and brave

'It takes a great deal of bravery to stand up to our enemies, but just as much to stand up to our friends.'

J. K. Rowling

Mastering assertiveness

Assertive people are comfortable expressing how they feel. They do not waffle, or feel obliged to justify, defend or explain their reasoning. They know their rights, they feel worthy, important and deserving. They are willing to be open and to compromise, as they do not always expect to get their own way. They have an 'I like you, but I like me too' approach. They are confident about handling conflict and they are able to give and receive positive and negative comments. They face the other person, look them in the eye, keep an open mind and demonstrate open body language. They watch their words, using 'could' and 'might' instead of 'should' and 'must'.

They feel competent and in control of themselves, and refuse to allow others to manipulate or control them. They always address issues as they arise, not a week or a month later. They are aware that they are 100% responsible for their own happiness and serenity. They place a high priority on having their rights respected, but they also respect the rights of others. They do not strut around with a sense of entitlement and the expectation that everyone will meet their needs, nor do they claim responsibility for how others think and feel. They own their actions and do not exhibit misplaced anger or inappropriate behaviour, but are clear, honest and to the point. Misplaced anger means that, if I am cross with my partner and haven't dealt with it, I will become angry at you at you if you happen to say the wrong thing. This is misplaced because it isn't about you; it is anger directed elsewhere that I haven't addressed.

The fundamentals of assertiveness

Assertive people consider their options and process things before replying to an email, text, question or remark. They do not deny a problem if there is one, and they do not smile when they are angry. They do not violate others' rights, nor do they make others afraid. They do not use language that shames other people or manipulate them into agreement. Neither do they act in a threatening or rude manner, or criticise others. They do not smile at you and then go behind your back. They never humiliate others or flag up their shortcomings, nor do they speak loudly or use 'you' statements.

> 'Confident people act and speak with certainty and boldness and if they don't like the road they are walking, they pave another one.'
>
> Dolly Parton

Assertive people are bold enough to take the risk, knowing that there may be a consequence. Assertive behaviour nearly always prompts respect from others, and the consequences are generally positive; however, some people can react negatively, especially if they have a huge ego or are used to getting their own way. Successful people know their bill of rights. I have taken this from my first book, *Doormat Nor Diva Be*.

YOUR BILL OF RIGHTS

- I have the right to express what I want and need.
- I have the right to set my own priorities and boundaries.
- I have the right to be treated with respect at all times.
- I have the right to express how I feel.
- I have the right to make mistakes.
- I have the right to change my mind at any time without feeling guilty.
- I have the right to express my uncertainty or confusion.
- I have the right to be treated as an intelligent and capable person.
- I have the right to decline responsibility for everyone else's problems.
- I have the right to express my opinions, thoughts and beliefs.
- I have the right to choose my own values and follow them.
- I have the right to say yes or no.
- I have the right to be who I am.
- I have the right to walk away if anyone shouts at me or talks down to me.
- I have the right to be valued and heard.
- I have the right to say it as it is.
- I have the right to own my power.
- I have the right to decide what is best for me.
- I have the right to like what I like without justifying, defending or explaining.

Maybe you want to ask your friend for the money back that you lent them, or you are upset about the way they trashed your flat when they house-sat? Maybe you have a tricky colleague at work, a business or romantic partner who is being unreasonable, or you have allowed your family members to take advantage of your kindness and now you feel a need to speak up?

By being assertive you are expressing your rights, feelings, needs, opinions and wants while having respect for the other person's feelings, needs, opinions and wants. You have basic human needs and the right to share your opinion, to ask for your needs and wants to be met. Successful people do not complain that others haven't met their needs or wants when they haven't asked them directly; they don't expect others to be mind-readers.

Establishing the different assertive styles

Principal assertion

- 'I need to leave by 4pm.'
- 'The cost is £50.'
- 'I would like time to think over what you have said.'

Compassionate assertion

- 'I recognise it's tricky to be exact about when you can get this back to me, but I need an approximate date.'
- 'I appreciate you do not like the boundaries I have put in place; however, while we are dating I would appreciate it if you could respect them.'

Incongruity assertion

- 'As I understand it, we agreed that x was top priority, and now you are asking me to give top priority to y. I therefore need to have clarity about what is now the top priority.'
- 'On the one hand, you say you want to improve communication between us, yet you come out with disrespectful remarks, which makes it difficult for me to believe that.'

Adverse assertion

- 'When you leave it so late to produce your progress report it means I end up going without lunch. I feel this is unfair, and therefore would appreciate it if I could receive it earlier.'

Consequence assertion (last resort)

- 'If you continue gambling I will be left with no choice but to leave you.'
- 'I am not prepared to be shouted at and spoken over, so I will make a formal complaint if this happens again, although I would prefer it not to get to that.'

Having suffered constant bullying at school from a young age and then as an adult in the workplace, I found it terrifying to be assertive for the first time, or to set boundaries, but it soon became very comfortable, and I can't imagine ever behaving in any other way. Once you have used these techniques and found those that work for you, and once you see the results they bring, I assure you that your confidence and self-esteem will rocket. Try tiny things to begin with and then, when you feel more comfortable, you can raise the bar.

Hostile, aggressive people display traits such as:

- arrogance
- being condescending
- being critical
- being demanding
- being judgemental
- being negative
- being over-opinionated
- being passive-aggressive
- blaming everyone else
- complaining
- egotism

- dictating
- showing off.

Those lacking confidence display traits such as:

- being all ideas but little action
- complaining behind others' backs
- indecisiveness
- lack of organisation
- not speaking up
- perfectionism
- procrastinating
- saying sorry too much
- saying yes too much
- taking everything personally
- talking too much
- using hedging words
- weak listening skills.

Identify your hotspots.

- What presses your buttons?
- Do you communicate clearly and assertively?
- Why do you react to certain people and situations?
- If you don't stand up for yourself, why not?
- What are your listening skills like?
- Are you aware of others' feelings and needs during moments of conflict?
- Are you aware of your non-verbal communication?
- Do you always look others directly in the eye when speaking?
- Do you paraphrase and use feedback during a conversation?
- When speaking with challenging people, do you suggest solutions or engage in drama?

Assertive techniques

Broken record

This is a simple yet effective technique: you keep repeating your request when dealing with unreasonable and difficult people who refuse to hear your point of view. For example, if a friend owes you £50 and hasn't paid you back, and suggests going to see a movie, you ignore the request for the movie to ensure you are not hooked in by them, and keep asking for your £50. The bottom line is that they are showing you a lack of respect, so you need to let them know you won't be taken for a fool and you want your money back. The key is repetition. This also works well if you want a refund and are not being taken seriously, or if someone is manipulative. Stay calm and focused and do not sway.

'I feel disrespected that you haven't paid me back my £50.'

'Sorry, it's been tricky lately with bills and so on. Let's have a laugh and go see a film on Friday.'

'I feel disrespected that you haven't paid me back my £50.'

Assertive inquiry

This technique means you don't talk just about the problem, but about how the other person is behaving at that moment. Maybe they are deflecting you with humour and skirting around the edges of what the problem is. Maybe they keep changing the subject or maybe they are not listening or taking you seriously. 'Whoa, let's hold this for a moment and look at how we got into this argument. Something isn't working.'

Defusing

It's always a good idea to refuse to discuss anything when someone is angry or shouting at you. It's always smart to suggest that they cool down or go for a walk and then you will discuss it. If they refuse and stand there behaving inappropriately, you have the right to walk away.

- 'I only respond when spoken to, not when shouted at.'
- 'It's unacceptable for you to keep interrupting. I am leaving as it is impossible to have a rational discussion while you keep butting in and speaking over me.'

DISC

This technique involves planning in advance on paper exactly what you would like to say.

- D = dare
- I = influence
- S = serenity
- C = consequences

You start by daring to be direct and honest, and describe the situation, problem or relationship issue. You influence in a non-manipulative way, describing your feelings and your needs. You must remember here that opinions are opinions, not facts, and they can be argued with. However, no-one can argue with how you feel, so it's important to distinguish this and be clear within yourself about it. You speak in a serene, rational way and keep a neutral tone, with direct eye contact, and you sit up or stand up. You deliver this message calmly by letting the other person know exactly what you feel uneasy, uncomfortable or upset about. You then conclude by telling someone that if they fulfil your needs, it will be a win–win situation and you explain the positive outcome.

Be specific and succinct: 'I feel sad we have this conflict in our department because I believe Suzie's disruptive behaviour prevents us from being more productive. I am convinced we could achieve more if we all worked together as a team.'

Fogging

Fogging deflects negative, manipulative, sarcastic remarks by agreeing with some of what is said while still owning your own power. It's very effective. Once the person knows that their remarks aren't bothering you, I promise you that they will quit. Generally, they want to provoke a reaction, so don't give it to them. If someone says 'You are lazy,' you can respond by saying: 'Yes, I can be lazy at times, and your point is?'

'You need to lose weight,' someone tells you. You reply, 'Yes, I am carrying some excess weight, and I love my curves.'

Successful, confident people have a commanding presence when they walk into a room. They listen to learn and learn to listen. They have learned the art of influence and persuasion without manipulation.

Be assertive, not aggressive

Assertiveness always comes from being super-confident. Aggressiveness always comes from lacking in confidence, and therefore being defensive, arrogant and having a sense of entitlement. Underneath super-confidence and assertiveness are heightened self-awareness, self-accountability, knowledge, wisdom, self-acceptance, self-love and self-belief.

My father always used to say that confident people don't lose their temper because they don't believe anyone is important enough to make them that angry. Read that over and over again.

Always follow the golden rules.

- **Use 'I' statements.** These are very powerful because they come from taking responsibility for yourself and speaking merely from your personal point of view and not blaming your feelings, thoughts or opinions on others.
- **State facts, not judgements.** Always label the behaviour, not the person. For example 'It's not OK for you to be unkind about my appearance'.
- **Use open body language.** Stand or sit straight. Your voice must be calm and gentle, but firm. Make direct eye contact.
- **Take ownership of how you feel.** Use statements such as, 'when you say xyz, I feel xyz '.

Good fences make good neighbours, right?

Good boundaries give you defined borders, and do not allow others to keep on taking. Boundaries are crucial, and assertive people always set and maintain them. If you want to learn to stand up for yourself, you need to have boundaries. These will help develop your emotional strength and build your confidence. First, you need to be clear about what your limits are. Perhaps you don't approve of someone smoking in your car. Perhaps you feel it is unacceptable for others to use bad language in front of your children. Perhaps you feel that your teenager is abusing your house by inviting friends over every night. Perhaps you feel it is not acceptable for your flatmate to constantly help herself to your milk in the fridge without asking. Perhaps a colleague keeps dumping extra work on you and assuming you will do it.

No-one has the right to abuse or disrespect you in any way. Sometimes people are so self-centred they are unaware that they are doing something to offend you, although others know exactly what they are doing and see you as a soft touch. By setting a boundary in an assertive way, you will form strong, more mutually respectful relationships, both professionally and personally, and will considerably raise your self-confidence. It's important that you respect other people's boundaries.

You get to decide

Setting boundaries illustrates that you have self-respect: it displays to others that you know yourself, and you know what is acceptable to you and what isn't. You know your own bottom line when you have boundaries.

> 'Understand you have the right to choose your own path, make your own choices about what works for you and what doesn't.'
>
> Oprah Winfrey

It is OK to set your own rules

By setting these boundaries and letting them be known through your assertive behaviour, you are stating what you feel are reasonable and permissible ways for others to behave around you and making it clear how you will respond if someone violates your boundaries. You need to learn to take care of yourself, and learn to be responsible for setting your own rules.

How many times have you allowed someone to treat you badly or manipulate you, and then *you* end up apologising and feeling guilty? People will not know that it is unacceptable to take advantage of you unless you tell them. When you have boundaries everyone knows where they stand; when you don't, those who don't have your best interests at heart, who are arrogant and egotistical, will often get angry and defensive when you dare to challenge their behaviour. And it's you who ends up feeling bad. This is what prevents many people from setting boundaries and being assertive.

Turn your thoughts around, turn your world around

Maybe you are over-reacting, being too sensitive, behaving childishly, being a drama queen or being unreasonable? No! If someone is being aggressive, manipulative, demanding, rude and arrogant, if they have expectations of you and a sense of entitlement, if they aren't contributing financially and aren't respectful to you, or if they put you down or jokingly show you up, *they* have the issue – *not you!*

Never be swayed or lose your footing. Remember: successful people are assertive and expect to be treated with respect because they respect themselves. They do not explain, justify or over-defend; they are direct and firm. If someone resists then keep repeating what you want to say, like a broken record. You must back up your boundaries by taking action and staying firm to take yourself seriously and have others take you seriously. Don't make your boundaries too rigid or too loose. This takes time and practice if you haven't done it before.

You are not responsible for the other person's reactions or responses to your boundaries. You will often find you are tested the first time you assert these boundaries, especially by those who are controlling you, abusing you or manipulating you for their own benefit. They won't like the new assertive, confident you. So remember that it's about you feeling happy and worthy, and raising your confidence and self-esteem.

> 'I will not allow anyone with dirty feet to walk through my mind.'
>
> Gandhi

Start giving to yourself what you give to others

You must ensure that you don't apologise when you set a boundary because this will send a mixed message and you won't be taken seriously. I am not promoting the attitude of 'My way or the highway,' here; I am suggesting you set a boundary that is respectful to you. Keep in mind that being Mr or Ms Nice not only means teaching others to trample all over you, but opening yourself up to allow others to get what they can from you without consideration – in other words, 'objectifying' you for their own purposes. Successful people do not search for approval, so they are not running around town wanting to be liked: they genuinely like themselves. Make yourself a priority; after all, when you're on a plane you are always asked to put your life jacket on first before you put on your child's. Think about it.

When setting your boundaries, think about the following questions.

- What are your values?
- What are your priorities?
- What is a deal-breaker for you?
- What are you happy to be more flexible about?
- When do you feel manipulated?

Are you taking care of your most valuable asset – you?

Do you feel angry when others make decisions for you, or when they have expectations that they have not discussed with you? Do you feel annoyed when someone spends your money for you, for instance, they decide where you are going on holiday, or where to eat when you are paying or splitting the bill? Does it anger you when someone borrows something of yours without asking? Do you feel that others are sarcastic, contemptuous or dismissive, making fun of you, and that when you pull them up they say that you are being too sensitive and that they were only joking?

These situations happen because other people consider that they are more important than you. You are agreeing by allowing it to happen. When you know what your bottom lines are, you won't impulsively say yes when you mean no and no when you mean yes.

'HALT'

Watch out for when you are hungry, angry, lonely or tired – HALT. These are the times when you are most vulnerable and when those who are manipulative, bossy, takers or self-centred can catch you off guard and press your buttons, so be prepared, and be clear about what is acceptable and what is not.

Most people admire boundaries because they then know where they stand with you. Ask for what you need in a way that shows you respect the other person. Give yourself permission to feel worthy of having boundaries. Not everyone will be co-operative, but you need to accept that. This technique is about building your courage muscles and raising confidence, so you shouldn't worry too much about the outcome; but remember that the practice itself is what will build your confidence and raise your self-esteem.

Boundaries are the limits of yourself and your responsibilities. You cannot control what others think of you, how they interact with or respond to you, but if you are unable to take care of yourself then you are giving others control over you.

Be like both an oak tree and a willow tree – rooted and grounded but flexible. Make your boundaries simple and direct.

Here are some examples.

- 'John, sorry; I am not comfortable lending money, but I am happy to help you develop a spending plan.'
- 'Mum, I would love to talk to you, but it doesn't work for me to speak after 9pm on week nights.'
- 'Janice, I find it unacceptable for you to swear in front of my children. Please refrain from doing so.'
- 'James, you need to go and watch TV downstairs for an hour. I need space. Please do not disturb me.'
- 'Mr Arnott, I would like to take Tuesday off, but I will ensure my work is covered.'
- 'Thank you for your opinion, but I am not comfortable with doing what you suggest and will do what feels right for me.'

Assertive people don't play games. They are honest in their interpersonal relationships and, because they are comfortable with themselves, they act in accordance with themselves. Those with no confidence act out on their feelings, while successful people verbalise them gently yet firmly, with no emotional charge. When you don't possess confidence, you don't feel you have the right to ask for what you need or to state how you feel. You are too concerned with what people will think of you, or whether you will be rejected or punished for having a different view or for saying no. You don't want to rock the boat or create a storm.

Another defence mechanism many use is 'projection'. This is when you are uncomfortable with your own shortcomings or limitations so you attribute them to someone else. It's also a common trait that you will dislike in others what you cannot see or accept in yourself. Those who lack confidence struggle to admit their flaws because they are ashamed by being anything other than perfect or flawless. Their ego, which focuses on 'less than' or 'better than', jumps into play.

Handling difficult people and difficult situations

Dealing with being bullied

Jennie, aged 37, is a sales manager in an IT firm in London. She is a bubbly, fun-loving, single mother. She initially came to see me for hypnotherapy to lose weight; however, after a few sessions, she burst out crying and told me she was being bullied at work by a female colleague.

First, her devious colleague befriended her so Jennie was totally unaware of her motives and subtly manipulative behaviour. She showed an interest in Jennie's life and invited her to social activities. She supported her close connection with their boss, who Jennie got on well with. Her colleague then started undermining her in front of other people and deliberately trying to trip her up by sending memos with incorrect information. Jennie decided to speak to her line manager and he suggested that she might be imagining it.

However, Jennie became more exasperated and felt powerless, and eventually she asked to speak to HR, who were really sympathetic but didn't offer any advice or resources. She wasn't sleeping, she was grumpy and irritable with her friends and her daughter, and she was absolutely fuming inside at the lack of support and the injustice. She started feeling mildly depressed.

Annie's thoughts. *I suggested that Jennie document every incident, record all remarks and conversations, and keep a copy of all emails, memos and correspondence. I told her to carry a notepad around at all times and, if anyone witnessed what was going on, to make a note of their name. Bullies excel at deception, manipulation and control. They will alter, deny or minimise any behaviour they are later pulled up on. They are masters at wriggling out of situations, and therefore manage to continue their aggressive behaviour by preying on others' fears.*

After several hypnotherapy sessions, learning the assertiveness techniques discussed in this book, practising role-playing and building her courage muscles, Jennie reported that her colleague had done a 360-degree turn and she was relieved beyond belief that she wasn't being tormented any more.

Many people have a great deal of fear about saying no and standing up for themselves at work, as they had it instilled in them while growing up, either at home or at school, that they must do what they are told.

Hazard warning

Watch out if anyone tries to get to know you quickly at work, because bullies often do this to figure out what your insecurities are and tap into your vulnerabilities. Some yell and act unprofessionally; some disguise their behaviour with charm. Often, you are a threat to bullies if you are talented, good-looking, successful, outgoing, popular and hardworking.

Remember: bullies always lack confidence and have low self-esteem, and they need to put others down to feel superior. Gentle approaches such as tolerance, logic, forgiveness, acceptance and being rational can occasionally stop mild bullying, but when a bully is relentless you need firmer tactics. This means having inner confidence, high self-esteem and assertiveness.

'I had a reading disability and was put into remedial classes and I felt excluded, and being small I was bullied a lot. I don't like bullies. People create their own life; it's about not running away but trying to see life in all its full glory.'
Tom Cruise

'I was in public school in Del Rio and I was sickly with asthma, kidney problems and ugly with buckteeth. I had no friends and a clique of middle-school girls kicked dirt on me while I was sitting under a tree eating a sandwich.'
Jessica Alba

Facts do not lie

Unfortunately, you can't make a legal claim directly about bullying, but complaints can be made under laws covering discrimination and harassment. However, if you are forced to resign due to bullying, then it's possible to make a constructive dismissal claim.

A survey by the Chartered Institute of Personnel and Development, the Trades Union Congress, the University of Manchester Institute of Science and Technology and Staffordshire University Business School in 2010 suggests around 14 million people in the UK are being bullied in the workplace. This is a shocking number, and it's painful to go through bullying. I have been there, and if you have as well, or if you know someone who has, then unless you or they possess inner confidence and use assertiveness techniques, it can erode confidence and cause your or their work, home life and even health to suffer.

'No' is a complete sentence

It may seem that I am contradicting what I said about listening and not interrupting, but if someone is being aggressive and refuses to listen to you saying no, then the effective, assertive approach is to say: 'I do apologise but I am going to interrupt you.'

Always use a sympathetic but firm tone when you say no. Always ensure that you are not too apologetic or start defending or justifying your response. Be firm and polite so the other person knows that you won't be manipulated into changing your mind.

You don't owe an explanation to anyone, so if you give one, give one from choice and not from obligation as I have done here. Once you start valuing your time and yourself, you will not want to please people and say yes when you mean no. Check your motive when you say yes instead of no; work out why you were dishonest to the person you were talking with, and with yourself. Be clear about what your priorities are and why you feel such a strong need to be nice all the time. If you struggle to say no at work, then explain to your boss that when you have too many commitments you may be unable to give each project the time and attention it deserves, and that this may weaken your productivity. If you feel uncomfortable to begin with, say you will respond in 24 hours. Get used to delaying your answer if you are a 'yes' person so that others no longer expect you to agree immediately; this will give them time to consider your situation or take you into account.

The power of the spoken word

Your thoughts create your reality, and when you are being assertive it is crucial to use words that express no doubt. Try changing:

- 'I think' to 'I know'
- 'I'll try' to 'I will'
- 'I'm not sure' to 'I am certain'
- 'maybe' to 'definitely'
- 'possibly' to 'I will confirm that'
- 'I may be wrong about that' to 'I am confident about that'
- 'I'll see' to 'I can' or 'I will'
- 'It's OK, it doesn't matter' to 'here's what I would like'.

Onwards and upwards

Meet Marcia

Marcia didn't consider herself important and, because she masked this, most people wouldn't have believed it to be the case. Years ago she had seen a therapist about her depression. From time to time she suffered from severe anxiety, and when she came to me she had hit rock bottom. She had limiting beliefs deep down.

- I need to kneel, cap in hand, to everyone – I am not as important as they are.
- Everyone else will be a success, but it won't happen for me.
- No-one listens to my opinion, because I am not important.

I don't actually think she was even aware of these beliefs until we talked things through and I challenged her. She told me her parents had been strict, she had always had to do as she was told, and she had felt unimportant because her views or opinions were not listened to. Marcia grew up believing that if she said no to partners or bosses, friends or colleagues, they would be angry, so she just agreed to go along with what they wanted, building up a lot of resentment on the way.

Marcia justified her actions, tried desperately to gain approval from others, strived to resolve everyone else's problems, and handed the lead over to everyone else. She gave into unreasonable demands from others time and time again, and she never dared give her opinion until someone else had given theirs. At work, Marcia was having projects dumped on her desk constantly. She tried every which way to communicate assertively and felt so frustrated at not being heard.

We worked out a communication style that made her feel important, confident and assertive, while staying authentic. We role-played and I helped her with influencing and persuasion skills and some NLP techniques for personal effectiveness. We also scripted a conversation that she needed to have with her boss to present her concerns. Things started to improve profoundly and people stopped taking advantage. See ya, Ms Naïve; hello, Ms Nifty.

How about you?

- What type of communication style do you feel you have?
- How do you feel others perceive you?
- Do you talk a lot or listen more?
- Do you ask questions?
- Do you lead or follow?
- Do you use the same style with everyone when having a conversation?

I am not suggesting you become a chameleon and mould yourself around what others want you to be. I am saying that by knowing your style, you can make others more comfortable and build a rapport, which is essential in the workforce. By selecting certain behaviours that fit you, it makes it simpler to resonate with other people.

The four basic styles

The four basic communication styles are:

1. passive
2. aggressive
3. passive-aggressive
4. assertive.

When we consider ourselves unimportant, we use either a passive or aggressive style of communication, and many swing between the two. For a moment, stop and think about yourself. Which of the following apply to you, and why might that be the case?

Limiting beliefs

- I cannot disagree, because then they may not like me.
- Everyone else is more important than me.
- I don't like to rock the boat.
- I am worthless.
- My contributions are not valuable.
- I couldn't tell them what I truly feel.
- Others can do things more effectively than me.
- I have no choice but to give in to unreasonable demands.
- If I go along with the crowd it will all be OK.
- I must not say anything that could attract comment or disapproval.

Communication style

- I tend to hesitate.
- I don't speak up.
- I am often indirect.
- I agree with others, to keep the peace.

Characteristics

- I allow others to make my decisions.
- I trust other people, but I don't trust myself.
- I am often apologetic for no reason.
- I don't ask for what I want or need.
- I minimise, alter and deny how I truly feel.
- I hide my pain by cracking jokes.
- I get embarrassed when someone praises me.
- I find it difficult to make decisions.
- I compromise my values to avoid anger or rejection.
- I judge myself harshly.
- I use indirect and evasive communication to avoid conflict or confrontation.

Behaviours

- I try to sit on both sides of the fence to avoid any confrontation.
- I ask permission unnecessarily.
- I put myself down frequently.
- I don't say what I need, want or feel.
- I let other people make the choices.

Verbal communication

- 'I couldn't do that but you would be amazing at it.'
- 'You are far more experienced than I am.'
- 'I could be wrong, but . . .'
- 'OK, I will try.'

Confrontation

- I often withdraw.
- I do anything to avoid conflict.
- I ignore phone calls or emails that are confrontational.
- I postpone meetings at work or with loved ones that are confrontational.

Non-verbal communication

- I fidget.
- I avoid eye contact.
- I sometimes hunch my shoulders.
- I often nod in agreement with colleagues when I don't agree.
- When I feel stressed and anxious, I speak too fast, and when I am feeling unsure, I speak slowly and quietly.

'I realised that conforming didn't accomplish anything. Do your own thing. As long as you learn that, you're cool.'

Sandra Bullock

Dr John Dewey says the deepest urge in human nature is the desire to be important. If you feel you are important, you will attract others who agree. Look around and spot those who do not feel important; they are generally the ones who are the most negative or cynical.

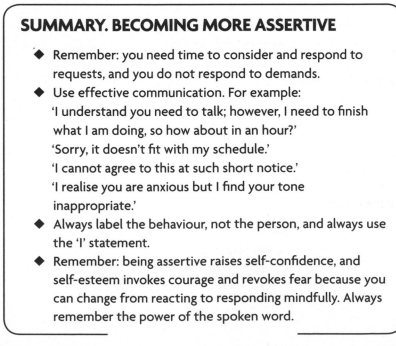

SUMMARY. BECOMING MORE ASSERTIVE

- ◆ Remember: you need time to consider and respond to requests, and you do not respond to demands.
- ◆ Use effective communication. For example:
  'I understand you need to talk; however, I need to finish what I am doing, so how about in an hour?'
  'Sorry, it doesn't fit with my schedule.'
  'I cannot agree to this at such short notice.'
  'I realise you are anxious but I find your tone inappropriate.'
- ◆ Always label the behaviour, not the person, and always use the 'I' statement.
- ◆ Remember: being assertive raises self-confidence, and self-esteem invokes courage and revokes fear because you can change from reacting to responding mindfully. Always remember the power of the spoken word.

◆ Put transformation into action by using effective techniques to deal with challenging people. Be aware of body language.

◆ Set boundaries, get familiar with your own bottom lines, set rules and be the one to make the decisions about how you run your life. Keep a copy of your bill of rights nearby or memorise it.

◆ Take advantage of opportunities by being assertive and taking control of your life.

A call to action

1. The lessons I have learned about self-assertiveness are:

....

....

2. A person or situation I have needed to be assertive around is:

....

....

3. I would like to start being more assertive because:

....

....

4. The excuses I might make to avoid asserting myself are:

....

....

5. The steps I will take to start being assertive are:

....

....

ANNIE'S CONFIDENCE-BOOSTERS FOR SELF-ASSERTIVENESS

- ◆ Decide what you need and ask for it.
- ◆ Have reasonable expectations of yourself and others.
- ◆ Use anger to be assertive (in a healthy way).
- ◆ Don't let anxiety build – take action now.
- ◆ Make requests simple and direct – no waffle.

A FINAL WORD

The promise

'Being realistic is the most common path to mediocrity.'
Will Smith

I hope that you are not too busy to process what is in this book or to complete the exercises, because they really can help you improve your life and boost your self-confidence. I promise you this: if you commit to change and use the tools in this book daily, you will not only build your confidence but your awareness will be so heightened that you will immediately recognise when you are slipping back into old attitudes, habits and behaviours. Bear in mind that you could still press the self-destruct button when things have improved, especially if your habit is to bring emotions into everything. Stay centred, practising the technique of sound emotional control so you can connect to your feelings while calmly expressing your needs and wants. If you neglect your needs, you will build up resentments that will blur your perception.

Remember to listen carefully to others, tap into your intuition and use your common sense by looking at the person or situation without the filters of your prior experience. Remember that you have choices and are worthy of asserting yourself, setting boundaries and saying no. Make sure your boundaries are reasonable, and remember your bill of rights and your right to be honoured, respected and valued.

Even if you have setbacks, stay willing to try new approaches and always bear in mind that other people's reactions are *their* issue, not yours. Steer clear of arrogant people and do not ever defend your choices, argue with them or waste time and energy trying to change their minds. Each of us has to accept his or her own inaction or action. If someone says something unkind, instead of reacting or allowing it to crush your confidence, take a step back, and have a good, honest look at yourself. Pull yourself out of self-absorption, eliminate self-pity and say to yourself: 'I am who I am, and I am more than enough.' Until you start being kind to yourself you cannot expect respect or consideration from others.

Giving up the need to be right and saying 'I may be wrong, you may be right,' will invigorate and empower you, making you comfortable with yourself and raising your self-confidence. When you use these tools, tips and techniques, life will become more interesting and productive and you will feel content within. You will allow others to live how they want without the impulse to judge and criticise, because you will have let go of judging and criticising yourself.

I hope that by reading this book you will have looked at yourself with love and respect, acknowledged the power that dwells within you, and begun to identify the values by which you want to live your life. I hope by self-examination you have gathered some valuable insights and begun to see the patterns of your behaviour to people and situations over the years. Whatever faults, habits, reactions and weaknesses you might have acquired, today you have freedom of choice to let them go if they no longer serve you.

My hope is that you begin to know who you are, to change the messages you tell yourself and to give yourself permission to stand up and shine. I would like you to find the peace and joy I have found with a clear mind and a steady heart. There is no magic formula, but I have shared with you how to get *The Confidence Factor.*

Go make it happen.

You can do it.

Annie

ABOUT THE AUTHOR

Annie Ashdown lives in Notting Hill Gate and is the author of *Doormat Nor Diva Be*. Since 2001 she has been working as a highly sought-after corporate trainer, business and personal development coach, motivational speaker, intuitive and energy healer, Louise Hay teacher and master hypnotherapist.

Annie designs and conducts one-day and weekend workshops focusing on the confidence factor and how to create an impact, in which she teaches the principles of assertiveness.

Recognising the tangible benefits of coaching and hypnotherapy, and having successfully applied them to her own situation after hitting rock bottom both personally and professionally, Annie decided after many years of being an entrepreneur and working in TV to change direction. Annie's clients include Vertu, Orange, Yahoo, Sky, ITV, Nokia, Google, the Royal Borough of Kensington and Chelsea, the Department for Work and Pensions, Jobcentre Plus, Business Link and Chelsea Football Club. Annie's individual clients include celebrities, barristers, police officers, scientists, diplomats, doctors, lawyers, bankers, designers, CEOs, teenagers, executive PAs, entrepreneurs, sales directors, business owners, psychotherapists and everyday people from all walks of life.

Annie's approach consists of a blend of proven metaphysical methods combined with spirituality. Annie appears on TV and features regularly in the press.

For further information, inspirational quotations, articles and training programmes, or to schedule a session with Annie, visit www.annieash-down.com. You can reach Annie directly by email at annie@annieash-down.com

A FEW OF ANNIE'S FAVOURITE INSPIRATIONAL QUOTATIONS

'I've finally stopped running from myself, who else is there better to be?'

Goldie Hawn

'I am so inadequate and I love myself.'

Meg Ryan

'Keep away from people who try to belittle your ambitions. Small people always do that, but the really great people make you feel that you too can become great.'

Mark Twain

'Surround yourself only with people who are going to take you higher.'

Oprah Winfrey

'Being confident is the sexiest thing.'

Kirsten Dunst

'Confidence is sexy to me. If a girl has confidence and self-esteem it definitely shows. Pretty is cool, but it's not really about looks for me. Confidence is the most attractive thing in the world.'

Justin Timberlake

'You can be true to the character all you want, but you've got to go home with yourself.'

Julia Roberts

'I like a girl who is confident.'

Jesse Metcalfe

'When I was younger, everyone must have assumed I was really spoilt as I had whatever trainers I wanted, and I earned every single penny. My old man never gave me hand-outs.'

Jamie Oliver

'It should be everyone's birthright to get the chance to fulfil their dreams. Yes, for some it's being a pop star. But for many more hard-working Brits, it's something far less flash — it's starting your own business.'

Simon Cowell

'Pessimism is an excuse for not trying and a guarantee for personal failure.'

Bill Clinton

'Personal happiness lies in knowing that life is not a checklist of acquisition or achievement. Your qualifications are not your life.'

J. K. Rowling

'I am just a girl from a trailer park who had a dream.'

Hilary Swank

'I do feel as an artist you need to go down before you can get up. That's definitely been good for me.'

Gary Barlow

'I think it's so important to believe in yourselves and believe in your empowerment and not wait for someone to rescue you and do it all for you. Go out there and create it all for yourself.'

Drew Barrymore

'Oh sure, I have lots of fears. My job is to conquer my fears. The irony of being a performer is that I have huge insecurities. Each of us is responsible for what happens in our lives. When good things happen, we take ownership, but when bad things happen we often don't take responsibility. There are no mistakes or accidents. Consciousness is everything and all things begin with a thought. We are responsible for our own fate. We reap what we sow, we get what we give and we pull in what we put out.'

Madonna

'You never really learn from hearing yourself talk.'

George Clooney

'Though I am grateful for the blessings of wealth, it hasn't changed who I am. My feet are still firmly on the ground. I am just wearing better shoes.'

Oprah Winfrey

'I quite like being who I am.'

Gary Barlow

'You simply have to be who you are. I have cellulite, don't be impressed with me. Don't spend your savings trying to be someone else. You are not more important, smarter or prettier because you wear designer dresses.'

Salma Hayek

'I have cellulite, I have stretch marks. Hollywood is one of those endless competitions. There's no winning. I accept myself and I just want to be the best version of myself I can be.'

Reese Witherspoon

'The world will ask who you are, and if you do not know, the world will tell you.'

Carl Jung

'Be true to yourself and everything will be fine.'

Ellen DeGeneres

'If I set my mind to something I do it. My biggest wish for all of us is that we are happy, successful and that we stay true to ourselves.'

Victoria Beckham

'Be yourself. Be a bigger yourself.'

Tyra Banks

'Always be a first-rate version of yourself instead of a second-rate version of someone else.'

Judy Garland

'Don't settle for a relationship that won't let you be your-self.'

Oprah Winfrey

'It's much better to be yourself than to try to be some version of what you think the other person wants.'

Matt Damon

'Don't compromise yourself, you are all you have got.'

Janis Joplin

'Your time is limited, so don't waste it living someone else's life. Don't be trapped by dogma — which is living with the results of someone else's thinking. Do not let the noise of other's opinions drown out your own inner voice.'

Steve Jobs

'Hard times arouse an instinctive desire for authenticity.'

Coco Chanel

'When you are real in your music, people know it and they feel your authenticity.'

Wynonna Judd

'The more I like me, the less I want to pretend to be other people.'

Jamie Lee Curtis

'To be one, to be united is a great thing. But to respect the right to be different is maybe even greater.'

Bono

'Have the courage to follow your heart and intuition, everything else is secondary.'

Steve Jobs

'The intellect has little to do with the road to discovery. The only real valuable thing is intuition.'

Albert Einstein

'You must train your intuition, you must trust the small voice inside you, which tells you exactly what to say and what to decide.'

Ingrid Bergman

'I am the girl who everyone said was never going anywhere. I guess I shocked a few people.'

Cher

'There is an expiry date on blaming your parents for steering you in the wrong direction. The moment you are old enough you need to take the wheel, as the responsibility lies within you.'

J. K. Rowling

'Live your life as an honest and compassionate person and contribute in some way.'

Ellen DeGeneres

'Every single negative can lead to a positive. Any negative situation ... don't get too down about it — you will work it out. You learn it as you go along. It will happen over time and it's the getting there which will be the most fun.'

Simon Cowell

'I encourage kids to never give up on their dreams. Take obstacles and make them the reason to have a big life.'

Orlando Bloom

'Belief in one's self and knowing who you are — that's the foundation for everything great.'

Jay-Z

'The most important thing in life is to live with integrity and not give into peer pressure, to try to be someone you are not.'

Ellen DeGeneres

'I do believe, and I have seen it in my own life, that creative visualisation works.'

Oprah Winfrey

'If you can dream it you can do it.'

Walt Disney

'I'm a very driven, ambitious, positive person. I'm a spiritual person as well and I believe in creative visualisation.'

Victoria Beckham

'The picture you have in your own mind of what you are about will come true.'

Bob Dylan

'We carry all the power we need inside ourselves already. We have the power to imagine. My parents took the view that my overactive imagination was an amusing quirk which would never pay a mortgage or secure a pension.'

J. K. Rowling

'We are each responsible for our own life. No-one else is or can be.'

Oprah Winfrey

'It is time to restore the American precept that each individual is accountable for his or her actions.'

Ronald Reagan

'I enjoy real people, down-to-earth people who are true to themselves and honest to your face — good or bad.'

Christina Aguilera

'Knowledge speaks but wisdom listens.'

Jimi Hendrix

'I will not allow anyone to walk through my mind with their dirty feet.'

Gandhi

'I realised that conforming didn't accomplish anything. Do your own thing. As long as you learn that, you're cool.'

Sandra Bullock

'Nothing is impossible; the word itself says I'm possible.'

Audrey Hepburn

'All dreams can come true if you have the courage to pursue them.'

Walt Disney

'They cannot take away our self-respect if we do not give it to them.'

Gandhi

'Success is the ability to go from one failure to another without a loss of enthusiasm.'

Sir Winston Churchill

'I trust everything happens for a reason, even if we are not wise enough to see it.'

Oprah Winfrey

'If you don't like the road you are walking, start paving another one.'

Dolly Parton

'Attitude is a little thing that makes a big difference.'
Sir Winston Churchill

'Be yourself, everyone else is taken.'

Oscar Wilde

FURTHER READING

Doormat Nor Diva Be by Annie Ashdown, Infinite Ideas.

Anyone Can Do It by Duncan Bannatyne, Orion.

Awaken the Giant Within by Anthony Robbins, Pocket Books.

Coco Chanel by Axel Madsen, Bloomsbury.

Creative Visualization by Shakti Gawain, New World Library.

Emotional Blackmail by Susan Forward, HarperCollins.

Emotional Freedom by Dr Judith Orloff, Crown.

Excuses Begone! by Dr Wayne Dyer, Hay House.

Guided Mindfulness Meditation by Jon Kabat-Zinn, Sounds True

Healing the Shame That Binds You by John Bradshaw, HCI.

How They Started by David Lester, Crimson.

How to Talk to Anyone, Anytime, Anywhere by Larry King, Crown.

I: Reality and Subjectivity by David R. Hawkins, Veritas.

Inspiring Women by Michelle Rosenberg, Crimson.

Losing My Virginity by Sir Richard Branson, Virgin.

Mandela: The Authorised Biography by Anthony Sampson, Harper Press.

Mindsight: The New Science of Personal Transformation by Daniel J. Siegel, Bantam.

Nonviolent Communication: A Language of Life by Marshall B. Rosenberg, Puddle Dancer Press.

Sixth Sense by Stuart Wilde, Hay House.

Strong Woman: Ambition, Grit and a Great Pair of Heels by Karren Brady, HarperCollins.

Sweet Revenge: The Intimate Life of Simon Cowell by Tom Bower, Faber and Faber.

Swim with the Sharks by Harvey Mackay, Sphere.

Tapping the Power Within by Iyanla Vanzant, Hay House.

The Dip by Seth Godin, Piatkus.

The Diving Bell and the Butterfly by Jean-Dominique Bauby, Fourth Estate.

The Four Agreements by Don Miguel Ruiz, Amber-Allen.

The Oprah Winfrey Story by Geraldine Woods, Dillon Press.

The Power Is Within You by Louise L. Hay, Hay House.

The Power of a Positive No by William Ury, Bantam.

The Power of Focus by Jack Canfield, Mark Victor Hansen and Les Hewitt, Vermilion.

The Power of Intention by Dr Wayne Dyer, Hay House.

The Power of Your Subconscious Mind by Dr Joseph Murphy, Wilder.

The Rules of Life by Richard Templar, Pearson.

The Success Principles by Jack Canfield, Element.

The Voice of Knowledge by by Don Miguel Ruiz, Amber-Allen.

The Vortex by Esther and Jerry Hicks, Hay House.

Train Your Mind, Change Your Brain by Sharon Begley, Ballantine.

War of the Worldviews: Science vs. Spirituality by Deepak Chopra and Leonard Mlodinow, Three Rivers Press.

Who Says I Can't? by Jothy Rosenburg, Bascom Hill.

You'll See It When You Believe It by Dr Wayne Dyer, Arrow.